EMPOWERED

THE BAPTISM IN THE HOLY SPIRIT

JOSHUA COPRON

ISBN: 9798282797268 (Copron)

DEDICATION

This book is dedicated to our Grace City Church family. We pray it helps you encounter the power of the Holy Spirit in a fresh way. May it be a tool that strengthens your faith, deepens your walk, and empowers you to live the Spirit-filled life God has made available to you.

THANKS

The baptism of the Holy Spirit is the gift that keeps giving. I wouldn't be who I am without it. Holy Spirit, this book exists because of what You've done in me—and I pray it helps others experience that same power, presence, and transformation. Thank You for the fire that never goes out.

INDEX

THE HOLY SPIRIT IS NOT A LUXURY; HE'S A NECESSITY.

INTRODUCTION

Years ago, a woman tried to rob a Howard Johnson hotel with a chainsaw—that's right, a chainsaw. She went into the front office with her power saw, but when she tried to turn it on, she realized there was a problem. It was an electric chainsaw.

But she wasn't going to let that stop her, so she started making a chainsaw noise herself, "heemmmmmm…give me all your money…heeemmmm…" Obviously, her attempt failed, and she was arrested. She had the equipment, but she was missing one important thing—power.

Like electric chainsaws, we were made to run on power. God designed us in such a way that we would need power. But not just any kind of power, divine power. Human beings were never meant to depend on human strength. We were created to be empowered by the Holy Spirit.

That is what the baptism in the Holy Spirit is; it's an empowerment from God that enables you to be everything God created you to be and do everything God created you to do.

The first chapter of Acts records Jesus' last words to His disciples before ascending into heaven.

And being assembled together with them, He commanded them not to depart from Jerusalem, but to wait for the Promise of the Father, "which," He said, "you have heard from Me; for John truly baptized with water, but you shall be baptized with the Holy Spirit not many days from now… But you shall receive power when the Holy Spirit has come upon you; and you shall be witnesses to Me in Jerusalem, and in all Judea and Samaria, and to the end of the earth."

ACTS 1:4-5, 8 (NKJV)

The word power in Greek is *dunamis*,[1] meaning divine ability and strength—the power to perform miracles, divine ability, and strength.

In Luke 24, this experience is described as being "clothed with power from on high" (Luke 24:49). The purpose of the baptism in the Holy Spirit is power. God never intended for us to handle the pressures of life on our own. He intended for us to be strengthened and empowered by the Holy Spirit.

In October 2018, Hurricane Michael swept through the panhandle of Florida and southwest Georgia, leaving a trail of destruction. Homes were damaged, trees uprooted, and entire communities lost power for weeks.

Thankfully, our house was fine—but we were stuck without power for weeks. I would have left town, but my wife and I stayed behind to help families in need. The problem was, without power, we couldn't keep the fridge cold, run the A/C, charge our phones, or even check social media to see if everyone was okay.

The worst part was that I kept forgetting that I didn't have power. I was at the house thinking, "Let's make something to eat..." Oh yeah, I can't cook anything. We don't have power. I went into the bathroom and tried to turn on the light. "Oh yeah, I don't have power." I turned on my computer and said, "I got some battery left," but I didn't have Wi-Fi, so I couldn't do anything.

I didn't realize how much my life was dependent on power. There were so many things I wanted to do, but I couldn't do them because I didn't have power. And that's exactly how many Christians feel. They want to live for God but lack the power to do it.

They see things in their life they want to change but feel powerless to change. They wrestle with temptations only to be defeated time and time again. There are unwanted habits they desire to be free from, but they lack the strength to overcome. They want to be used by God to make a difference but all their efforts seem to yield no results.

If they could describe their lives in one word, it would be powerless. But you don't have to be powerless. You don't have to experience constant defeat. You can walk in supernatural strength. You can be equipped with the divine ability to overcome every obstacle and barrier that stands in your way and be empowered to fulfill God's purpose for your life.

Jesus said, "You shall receive power when the Holy Spirit comes upon you." The baptism in the Holy Spirit is a baptism of power that enables you to tap into God's supernatural strength, ability, and miracle-working power.

It enables you to conquer obstacles with greater ease. It equips you with miracle-working power, and it empowers you to fulfill your purpose.

THE NEW TESTAMENT MENTIONS THREE DIFFERENT BAPTISMS WE ARE TO EXPERIENCE.

CHAPTER 1

THREE BAPTISMS

One day I was having lunch with a man named Robert. He told me how different our church was from the denomination he grew up in—but in a good way. He was thankful for how much the church had helped him.

Then he said, "But there's one thing that's strange. Why do you always call it 'water baptism?' We always just called it 'baptism.'"

I said, "Because there's more than one baptism in scripture."

He gave me a confused look, like he'd never heard that before. So I told him what I'm about to share with you.

Hebrews 6 mentions the foundational principles of the faith, and one of the foundations mentioned is "the doctrine of baptisms" (Hebrews 6:1-3). What's interesting about Hebrews is that it says "baptisms," not "baptism." It's plural, not singular because there is more than one baptism.

The word *baptism* [1] means to dip, immerse, or submerge. For us, this word carries religious connotations, but it was part of the common vocabulary of the first century.

Have you ever dropped your phone in a pool? If so, your phone was baptized—and it probably cost you a lot of money. Have you ever dropped your phone in the toilet? At that moment, you have a decision to make: Do I grab it as quickly as possible with my hand, or do I just give up and scoop it out with something else and get a new phone? Either way, that phone has been baptized—completely immersed.

This word describes anything being dipped, immersed, or submerged. The New Testament mentions three different baptisms that we are to experience.

BAPTISM IN CHRIST

The first baptism we experience as believers happens the moment we give our lives to Christ. The moment you become a follower of Jesus, you are baptized into Christ.

> For by one Spirit we were all baptized into one body.
> 1 CORINTHIANS 12:13 NKJV

The one body we are baptized into is the body of Christ. Romans 5 describes how all the world is either "in Adam" or "in Christ." When you came to faith in Jesus, you were taken out of Adam and placed into Christ.

Throughout the New Testament, the phrase "in Christ" or "in Him" defines your identity. Being baptized into Christ means that God relates to you not on the basis of your performance but your position in Christ. Your identity is determined by the fact that you are in Christ.

BAPTISM IN WATER

Water baptism is the next step after salvation. It's not what saves us—faith in Jesus alone does that—but it is the first act of obedience in following Him. Scripture is clear: belief comes first, and baptism follows.

"Whoever believes and is baptized will be saved..."
MARK 16:16 NKJV

In Acts 2:38, Peter calls the crowd to "Repent, and be baptized..." This wasn't a suggestion or an optional follow-up. It was a direct response to the Gospel. Water baptism is the outward expression of the inward transformation that has already taken place.

For we died and were buried with Christ by baptism. And just as Christ was raised from the dead... now we also may live new lives.
ROMANS 6:4 NKJV

Baptism is a beautiful picture of what Jesus has done for us. It connects us to His death, burial, and resurrection. It's how we say, "I'm leaving the old life behind and stepping into everything God has for me." (Romans 6:4)

BAPTISM IN THE HOLY SPIRIT

The majority of Christians agree with the first two baptisms, but the baptism in the Holy Spirit remains controversial for some reason, even though it's clearly talked about all through the New Testament.

John answered them all, "I baptize you with water. But

one who is more powerful than I will come, the straps of whose sandals I am not worthy to untie. He will baptize you with the Holy Spirit and fire."

LUKE 3:16 NKJV

John describes Jesus as the one who will baptize us in the Holy Spirit. So Jesus is the one who performs this baptism, and the medium that He immerses us into is the Holy Spirit.

All four gospel writers introduce us to Jesus as the one who will baptize us in the Holy Spirit (Matthew 3:11; Mark 1:8; Luke 3:16; John 1:33). This isn't some side thing Jesus does—it's central to the ministry of Jesus.

Interestingly, during His earthly ministry, Jesus didn't baptize anyone in the Holy Spirit. He preached the Kingdom, healed the sick, cast out demons, raised the dead, but he didn't baptize anyone in the Spirit.

> **This baptism isn't some afterthought— it's essential to Jesus' ministry.**

After His resurrection, Jesus told His disciples to wait in Jerusalem to be baptized in the Holy Spirit (Acts 1:4-9). Then on the day of Pentecost, the 120 disciples were baptized in the Holy Spirit (Acts 2:1-4).

The baptism in the Holy Spirit is a part of the current ministry of the ascended Christ. What's interesting is that many people are followers of Jesus, and yet they reject this present-day ministry of Jesus.

This baptism isn't some afterthought—it's essential to Jesus' ministry. We don't talk about Jesus as the baptizer. We talk about Jesus as Savior, Redeemer, Healer, and Deliverer—but He is also the one who baptizes us in the Holy Spirit.

This particular phrase, "the baptism in the Holy Spirit," is specifically mentioned six times in the New Testament, but the Bible uses various phrases to describe the same experience.

The New Testament describes this experience in various ways: "baptized with the Holy Spirit" (Acts 1:5), "filled with the Holy Spirit" (Acts 2:4), and "received the Holy Spirit" (Acts 19:2). Other expressions include "the Holy Spirit came upon" (Acts 1:8), "the gift of the Holy Spirit" (Acts 2:38), "poured out the Holy Spirit" (Acts 2:33), "the Holy Spirit fell upon" (Acts 10:44 NASB), "clothed with power from on high" (Luke 24:49), "anointed with the Holy Spirit" (Acts 10:38), and "received the promise of the Holy Spirit" (Acts 2:33). These terms highlight the same experience—being immersed in the Spirit of God.

If Jesus is the one who baptizes us in the Holy Spirit, then why settle for anything less than everything He came to give?

GOD WANTS YOU TO BE IMMERSED IN THE HOLY SPIRIT IN SUCH A WAY THAT YOU ARE CHANGED FOREVER.

CHAPTER 2

GET PICKLED

I love cookies. When my wife and I first got married, we had freshly baked cookies every single night. She would make a batch of cookie dough at the start of the week, and each night, we'd pop a batch in the oven. There's nothing like the smell of warm, fresh-baked cookies filling the house.

They say when you go to college, you put on the "Freshman Fifteen." Well, when I got married, I put on the "Newlywed Nineteen." I blame the cookies.

One night, though, things didn't go according to plan. My wife baked the cookies, and when we pulled them out of the oven, they were flat and burnt. That's when she realized she'd skipped a step in the process: she forgot to add baking powder. Now, I'm no baking expert, but I learned that night that skipping baking powder is a big deal. It's not a minor detail. Without it, the cookies don't rise, and they certainly don't taste like they're supposed to.

That little misstep ruined the entire batch. One small omission made a big difference.

The same is true in our faith. God designed a process for our growth—three key steps: salvation, water baptism, and baptism in the Holy Spirit. Skip a step, and the results won't be what God intended.

The same is true in our faith. God has designed a process for us—a series of steps to help us grow, thrive, and be empowered to live out His purpose. If we skip any of these steps, it's like leaving out the baking powder: the results won't be what God intended.

Just as baking powder is crucial to cookies, all three baptisms—baptism into Christ, water baptism, and the baptism in the Holy Spirit—are crucial to our spiritual growth. Each plays a vital role in shaping us into the people God designed us to be. Let's not skip any steps, because when we follow His full plan, the results are life-changing.

Each baptism is an essential step in God's process of transforming our lives—which is why all three are illustrated in what scholars refer to as *types and shadows* throughout the Old Testament.

Think of "types and shadows" as previews or symbolic pictures—real events or people in the Old Testament that point to deeper spiritual truths fulfilled in the New Testament. They're like a movie trailer: not the full story, but enough to show you what's coming.

> For I do not want you to be ignorant of the fact, brothers and sisters, that our ancestors were all under the cloud and that they all passed through the sea. They were all baptized into Moses in the cloud and in the sea.
>
> 1 CORINTHIANS 10:1-2 NIV

Notice the verse says they were baptized into three things: Moses, the sea, and the cloud. Moses, for the Jewish people, was their deliverer. He was the one who went in so they could come out. Moses is a prophetic picture of Jesus, our deliverer, who came in to bring us out.

Then they passed through the sea. The Egyptian army followed them, but the waters came down and swallowed them up, leaving Egypt behind in the water. This is a picture of water baptism—leaving behind our old life and stepping into the freedom God provides.

Then it says they were baptized in the cloud. When the Israelites came out of Egypt, they were under the cloud by day and the pillar of fire by night that led them through the wilderness. That cloud represents the Holy Spirit's presence—just as we are led by the Spirit today.

So they were baptized into Moses—salvation, the sea—water baptism, and the cloud—the Holy Spirit. The foreshadowing of these three baptisms is also found in the ritual of the Tabernacle in the Old Testament.

Before the priests ministered in the Tabernacle, they followed three steps. First, they went to the bronze altar and sacrificed an animal, shedding its blood (Exodus 29:10-14), which represents Jesus' sinless sacrifice for the forgiveness of sins (John 1:29).

Next, they went to the bronze basin (Exodus 30:17-21) and washed in the water, which signified water baptism (Romans 6:3-4).

Finally, the priests would be anointed with oil before ministering (Exodus 29:7). Oil represents the anointing of the Holy Spirit, which empowers us for ministry and service (1 Samuel 16:13).

These three elements—blood, water, and Spirit—are all present in the Tabernacle rituals and have symbolic connections in the New Testament. 1 John 5 refers to these three elements.

For there are three that testify: the Spirit, the water and the blood; and the three are in agreement.

1 JOHN 5:7-8 NKJV

Notice, all three elements—blood, water, and oil—were used in the consecration and purification of the Old Testament priests and are mirrored in New Testament themes of salvation, baptism, and the Holy Spirit's anointing.

God's intention is for us to experience all three baptisms—so we can fully receive what He has for us and be empowered to fulfill His calling.

EXAMPLE OF JESUS

Even Jesus experienced all three baptisms—well, sort of. Obviously, He didn't need salvation because He is the Christ. He didn't need to be saved because He was born of the Spirit (Luke 1:35). However, Jesus went to the Jordan River to be baptized by John. When He came out of the water, the Spirit of God descended upon Him like a dove (Matthew 3:16). So Jesus was baptized in water and anointed with the Holy Spirit.

Before the Spirit descended upon Jesus, He did not start His ministry or do any miracles. It wasn't until He was immersed in the Spirit that He began His ministry and started performing miracles because the Holy Spirit empowered the ministry of Jesus.

> God anointed Jesus of Nazareth with the Holy Spirit and with power, who went about doing good and healing all who were oppressed by the devil, for God was with Him.
>
> ACTS 10:38 NKJV

When Jesus came out of the water, He was anointed with the Holy Spirit and power. Then He went about doing good and healing the oppressed.

If the sinless Son of God needed the empowerment of the Holy Spirit to accomplish His ministry, why would we think we can be effective without it?

If Jesus needed the anointing of the Holy Spirit to fulfill His ministry, how much more do we need the Holy Spirit's power to do what God has called us to do?

THREE DISTINCT EXPERIENCES

Some people say that the baptism in the Holy Spirit is the same as being baptized in Christ. They believe these two phrases refer to the same experience which happens when you are saved.

But you don't need a theology degree to understand that it's not the same thing. A basic understanding of grammar will reveal that these are three distinct experiences.

When you read the word grammar, you probably thought you would have to remember something from high school English but you don't. Mainly because I don't remember anything from English class, I think it's because I got off to a rough start at school.

My mom didn't tell me anything about school. She just said, "Get in there…they'll feed you in a little while."

I didn't know what was going on when they started teaching me the alphabet. I thought they were reading off the lunch menu. "A—is for apple. B—is for banana (Nah). C—is for Cake (okay). D—is for dog." What kind of place is this?

I was confused in kindergarten, for sure. But it didn't help when they told me that I would learn the three R's in school: reading, writing (that's your second R), and arithmetic (that's your third R). I said, "Hey, I know I'm new here, but what about Rocial studies or Ristory and Reography? Was Scooby-Doo the commissioner of education? Rets read some rooks!"

You don't need an English degree to recognize that these three baptisms are separate and distinct experiences. A basic understanding of grammar makes it clear.

Baptism in Christ – The Holy Spirit immerses you in Christ.

Water Baptism – A fellow believer immerses you in water.

Baptism in the Holy Spirit – Jesus immerses you in the Holy Spirit.

The person performing the baptism and the medium into which you're immersed are different in each case. These three baptisms are separate experiences, each with a distinct purpose.

The first baptism gets you into heaven. You do not need any of the other baptisms to be saved. The first baptism is the only one necessary for salvation.

But just because the other two aren't necessary for salvation doesn't mean they're optional. They are required for other reasons. Water baptism brings deliverance from your old life, and the baptism in the Holy Spirit is necessary for power.

Unfortunately, many people stop at water baptism. However, just as you were baptized in water, God wants you to be baptized in the Holy Spirit. When you were baptized in water, you were completely immersed in water. When a person is baptized in the Holy Spirit, they are completely immersed in the Spirit of God.

GETTING PICKLED

The Bible uses two Greek words to describe immersion: *baptó*[1] and *baptizó*.[2] One of the earliest ancient writings to use these terms is a recipe for making pickles.

You know you can't grow pickles, right? You have to make them. You can't buy pickle seeds and grow pickles. God never said in Genesis, "Let there be pickles!"

Pickles are just cucumbers that have been through a process. The Greek poet and physician Nicander used *baptó* and *baptizó* in a recipe for making pickles.[3]

To make a pickle, you first blanch the cucumber in boiling water, which softens the skin. Then you immerse it in a vinegar solution and seal the jar. Over time, the vinegar penetrates the cucumber, changing it from a cucumber to a pickle.

In this ancient recipe for making pickles, the word *baptó* refers to the initial act of dipping a vegetable in boiling water and the word *baptizó* describes the subsequent immersion in vinegar.

When you were baptized in water, you were *baptó'd.* You were dipped into the water, and then you came out. However, God's desire for you goes beyond this initial act; He wants you to be *baptizó'd*—fully immersed in the Holy Spirit.

God wants you to move from being dunked in the waters of baptism to being pickled in the Holy Spirit. He wants you to be immersed in the Holy Spirit in such a way that you are changed forever.

God wants you to be enveloped in the Holy Spirit to such a degree that it completely changes your life.

THE OUTPOURING OF THE HOLY SPIRIT WASN'T RANDOM—IT WAS PERFECTLY TIMED WITH THE FEAST OF PENTECOST.

CHAPTER 3

PASSOVER & PENTECOST

Have you ever heard a "how many does it take to change a light bulb" joke? Like, how many CrossFitters does it take to change a light bulb? Three—one to do it in record time, one to film it, and one to complain about proper form.

Let's try some denominational light bulb jokes. Don't worry—I'll make fun of everyone equally:

How many Presbyterians does it take to change a light bulb? None. The lights will go on and off at predestined times.

How many Charismatics does it take to change a light bulb? One—their hands are already in the air.

How many Church of Christ members does it take? None—light bulbs aren't mentioned in the New Testament; therefore, they are unscriptural.

How many United Methodists does it take? We choose not to make a statement either in favor of or against the need for a light bulb. However, if in your own journey, you have found that light bulbs work for you, you are invited to write a poem or compose a modern dance about your light bulb for next Sunday's service, in which we will explore several light bulb traditions, including incandescent, fluorescent, and LED, all of which are equally valid paths to luminescence.

How many Baptists does it take? Change?! Who said anything about change?

How many Pentecostals does it take? Ten—one to change the bulb and nine to bind the spirit of darkness.

Pentecostal is considered a denomination, but it's really not a denomination. The word *Pentecost* comes from the Greek word for fiftieth.

I know that might come as a shock to some people. They think it means speaking in tongues, snake handling, wild worship, with people dancing like those air tube men you see outside a car dealership.

But it simply means fifty because the Feast of Pentecost was fifty days after Passover. Fifty days after Jesus rose from the dead, the Holy Spirit was poured out on the day of Pentecost.

Pentecostals simply believe that what happened on the day of Pentecost is still available today. They believe that in the same way the disciples were baptized in the Holy Spirit, you can be baptized in the Holy Spirit.

They're called Pentecostals because the Holy Spirit was poured out on the day of Pentecost. If the Holy Spirit had been poured out on Christmas, they'd be called Christmas-costals. If it happened on Easter, they'd be Easter-costals. But since it happened on Pentecost, they're Pentecostals.

People often ask if our church is a Pentecostal church. If by that you mean snake handling, tambourines, shofars, and ladies with really long skirts and no makeup, or ladies with a whole lot of makeup—then no.

But if you mean that the same experience the disciples had in the upper room is available to believers today, then yes, we are a Pentecostal church. We believe that what God did then, He still does today. The same baptism the 120 experienced on Pentecost is available for every believer today.

Now, the baptism in the Holy Spirit is a controversial topic. What people believe about the Holy Spirit and His work in our lives has been a major source of division in the church. Some denominations believe the baptism in the Holy Spirit is a separate experience after salvation, while others believe you receive it the moment you give your life to Christ.

Let's examine what the Word of God teaches about this subject. Is the baptism in the Holy Spirit something you receive at salvation, or is it a separate experience that happens after salvation?

When you read through the New Testament, it's clear that there are two distinct ways people experience the Holy Spirit. These two ways are illustrated through two Sundays: Resurrection Sunday and Pentecost Sunday.

On both Sundays, believers had an encounter with the Holy Spirit—but the experiences were different.

RESURRECTION SUNDAY

In John 20, Jesus had already died and risen from the grave. He appeared to His disciples and said, "Hey, y'all!" (That's the South Georgia translation). He showed them the holes in His hands and side.

So Jesus said to them again, "Peace to you! As the

Father has sent Me, I also send you." And when He had said this, He breathed on them, and said to them, "Receive the Holy Spirit."
JOHN 20: 21-22 NKJV

In Greek, the words for *breath* and *spirit* are the same, so Jesus breathed on them and said, "Receive the Holy Spirit." The word used here for *breathed* is *emphysaō*,[1] which means to breathe into or to inflate. It's the same word used in the Septuagint (the Greek translation of the Old Testament) in Genesis 2:7 when God breathed into Adam the breath of life at creation.

There are two distinct ways people experience the Holy Spirit.

Just as God breathed life into mankind at creation, Jesus breathed into His disciples, and they received the Holy Spirit.

At this moment, the disciples experienced New Testament salvation. They had already confessed Jesus as Lord, but this was the first time they believed in His resurrection. Scripture says that to be saved, you must confess with your mouth that Jesus is Lord and believe in your heart that God raised Him from the dead (Romans 10:9).

To be saved, you must confess with your mouth that Jesus is Lord and believe in your heart that God raised Him from the dead. These disciples confessed Jesus as Lord before, but this is the first time they believed God raised Him from the dead.

At this point, they passed from death to life; at this moment, they experience eternal life, and they receive the indwelling Holy Spirit. Before this, they walked in faith like all believers in the Old Testament, but now they've seen Christ and received the indwelling Holy Spirit.

Before this moment, no one besides Jesus had the Holy Spirit *living in them*. The Holy Spirit was with people and *came* upon people in the Old Testament, but He didn't dwell *in* them. For the first time, the Holy Spirit took up residence in the believer. Because of the cross and resurrection, we can now experience the indwelling of the Holy Spirit. Because of the finished work of the cross, the Holy Spirit now resides in us.

This is the resurrection Sunday experience with the Holy Spirit. This happens every time someone gives their life to Christ—they pass from death to life, and the Holy Spirit comes to live inside them.

PENTECOST SUNDAY

Now that the disciples have seen Christ and received the Holy Spirit, do they rush to tell everyone that Jesus is alive? No, instead of telling them to go, Jesus told them to **wait**.

Jesus' last words to His disciples are recorded in Acts 1. As soon as He finished speaking, He ascended to heaven—so you know His final instructions were important.

Jesus was getting ready to turn over the hope of the world to his disciples, so his final words are vital to the success of the Great Commission. What He tells them in this moment will ensure that the baton is passed to the next generation and not dropped.

> And being assembled together with them, He commanded them not to depart from Jerusalem, but to wait for the Promise of the Father, "which," He said, "you have heard from Me; for John truly baptized with water, but you shall be baptized with the Holy Spirit not many days from now."
>
> ACTS 1:4-5 NKJV

The same group of people Jesus had already breathed on and said, "Receive the Holy Spirit," were now told to wait until they were baptized in the Holy Spirit.

They had the Holy Spirit living *in* them, but they needed to wait until the Holy Spirit came *upon* them.

I'm sure they were wanting to go and tell everyone about Jesus—but they weren't ready yet. They didn't have the power they needed to accomplish the Great Commission.

It's great to believe in Jesus, receive forgiveness, and have the Holy Spirit living in you—but there's more you need. You need the baptism in the Holy Spirit. In Acts 1:8, Jesus told them exactly why they needed this second experience with the Holy Spirit:

"But you shall receive power when the Holy Spirit has come upon you; and you shall be witnesses to Me in Jerusalem, and in all Judea and Samaria, and to the end of the earth."
ACTS 1:8 NKJV

The disciples already had the Holy Spirit *in them*, but Jesus said they would receive power when the Holy Spirit came *upon them*. The Holy Spirit lives *in you* at salvation, but He comes *upon you* when you are baptized in the Holy Spirit.

They received the Holy Spirit when Jesus breathed on them—but 50 days later, the Holy Spirit came upon them.

"When the Day of Pentecost had fully come, they were all with one accord in one place. And suddenly there came a sound from heaven, as of a rushing mighty

> wind, and it filled the whole house where they were sitting. Then there appeared to them divided tongues, as of fire, and one sat upon each of them. And they were all filled with the Holy Spirit and began to speak with other tongues, as the Spirit gave them utterance."
>
> ACTS 2:1-4 NKJV

The same people Jesus breathed on to receive the Holy Spirit in John 20 were now baptized in the Holy Spirit in Acts 2. As you can see from their experience, the baptism in the Holy Spirit is a separate experience from receiving the Holy Spirit at salvation.

Resurrection Sunday was about salvation and the indwelling of the Spirit. Pentecost Sunday was about empowerment and the outpouring of the Spirit. Pentecost doesn't contradict Resurrection Sunday—it completes it. They fit together perfectly. It's not either-or; it's both.

When you gave your life to Christ, the Holy Spirit came to live inside of you. Imagine you are holding an empty cup. This represents your life before Christ; it's empty, but when you give your life to Jesus, your empty cup is filled with the Holy Spirit. This is what happens when you get saved.

This cup has been filled, but it hasn't been baptized. When you are baptized in the Holy Spirit you are immersed in the Spirit of God. If you took the filled cup and immersed it in a pitcher of water, the cup would be full and completely covered. This is what happens when you are baptized in the Holy Spirit. The Spirit fills you and completely covers you.

PASSOVER

These two experiences with the Holy Spirit not only revolve around two Sundays but also two major feasts in the nation of

Israel. Understanding the nature of each feast helps reveal the distinct difference between the indwelling and the empowering work of the Holy Spirit.

God instituted three major feasts for the nation of Israel: the Feast of Passover, the Feast of Pentecost, and the Feast of Tabernacles.

The Feast of Passover is one of the most significant Jewish festivals, commemorating God's deliverance of the Israelites from slavery in Egypt.

The Israelites had been enslaved in Egypt for centuries. God, through Moses, demanded that Pharaoh release them, but Pharaoh refused—leading to a series of plagues. The tenth and final plague was the death of all the firstborn in Egypt.

Passover represents the work of salvation.

To spare the Israelites from this plague, God instructed them to sacrifice a spotless lamb, apply its blood to the doorposts of their houses, and eat a meal prepared with unleavened bread. The blood would serve as a sign for the Angel of Death to "pass over" their homes, sparing their firstborn.

That night, the firstborn of the Egyptians—from Pharaoh's household to the lowest servant—died, while the Israelites were spared. This final plague convinced Pharaoh to release the Israelites.

The next day, the Israelites left Egypt in a mass exodus, marking the beginning of their journey to the Promised Land. God commanded the Israelites to observe the Passover every year to remember how He saved them from slavery (Exodus 12:14).

Passover was a foreshadowing of Jesus Christ's sacrifice. Jesus is referred to as the *Lamb of God* (John 1:29). He was crucified during Passover, and His blood was shed to deliver us from the slavery of sin and death (1 Corinthians 5:7). And He was raised from the dead on the last day of Passover—Resurrection Sunday.

Just as the Israelites were freed from Egypt by the blood of the lamb, we are freed from sin by the blood of Christ. Passover represents the work of salvation. The moment you put your faith in Jesus, you experience your personal Passover. The blood of the Lamb delivers you from sin and brings you into new life.

Salvation makes you ready for heaven, but there's more. God doesn't just want to save you—He wants to empower you. That's why the story doesn't end with Passover; it leads to Pentecost.

PENTECOST

The Feast of Pentecost occurred 50 days after Passover. Pentecost was originally an agricultural festival marking the end of the grain harvest, where they offered their first fruits to God. It also commemorated the giving of the Law at Mount Sinai—making it both a harvest festival and a celebration of God's covenant.

It's no coincidence that the Holy Spirit was poured out on the day of Pentecost. Just as God used the timing of Passover to communicate the significance of the cross and resurrection, He used the timing of Pentecost to communicate the purpose of the baptism in the Holy Spirit.

The outpouring of the Spirit at Pentecost happened at the end of the harvest season. Jesus often used the analogy of a harvest to describe reaching the lost and how people were ready to receive the Good News.

> "Open your eyes and look at the fields!
> They are ripe for harvest."
> JOHN 4:35 NKJV

In Revelation, Jesus is depicted holding a sickle—a tool used for harvesting—symbolizing the gathering of souls at the end of the age (Revelation 14:15).

God is referred to as the *Lord of the harvest*, and the church is the sickle in His hand. We are the ones God uses to reach the lost. The Holy Spirit was poured on the day of Pentecost to empower us to go into all the world, preach the Gospel, and reach the lost. We cannot bring in the harvest without the power of the Holy Spirit.

Just as Pentecost in the Old Testament celebrated the harvest of first fruits, in the New Testament, it symbolizes the spiritual harvest—and the empowerment of the Holy Spirit for ministry.

But Pentecost didn't just celebrate the end of the harvest season but also the giving of the Law.

In Exodus 32, Moses went up the mountain and received the Ten Commandments from God. When Moses came down the mountain with the Ten Commandments, all the people worshipped the golden calf. Moses said, "Whoever is on God's side stay over here and everyone else move over there." Then, they killed everyone who wasn't on the Lord's side. And it says, "About 3,000 died that day" (Exodus 32:28 NLT).

At the coming of the law, about 3,000 died. But on the Day of Pentecost, when the 120 were gathered together in the upper room and the Holy Spirit was poured out, Peter got up and preached, empowered by the Holy Spirit, and scripture says, "About 3,000 were saved that day" (Acts 2:41 NIV).

At the giving of the Ten Commandments, *3,000 died.* At the coming of the Spirit, *3,000 were saved.*

At the first Pentecost, Moses came down with the Law written on tablets of stone. At Pentecost in Acts 2, God wrote His law on the people's hearts through the Holy Spirit—fulfilling the promise of Jeremiah 31:33 and Ezekiel 36:26–27—that He would put His Spirit within us and empower us to follow Him.

Passover brought salvation; Pentecost brought empowerment. The Spirit in you makes you a child of God. The Spirit upon you empowers you to represent Him as a child of God.

COMPARE AND CONTRAST

As you can see, each feast and each experience with the Holy Spirit serves a separate and unique purpose.

At Passover, the disciples saw the resurrected Christ. At Pentecost, they experienced the direct ministry of the ascended Christ. On Passover, Jesus breathed on His disciples and said, "Receive the Holy Spirit." On the day of Pentecost, the Holy Spirit came upon them.

When Jesus appeared to His disciples on Resurrection Sunday, He said, "Peace be with you" (John 20:19). The result of salvation is peace with God. But when Jesus told His disciples to wait in Jerusalem, He promised they would receive power when the Holy Spirit came upon them (Acts 1:8).

It wasn't enough for the disciples to have peace—He wanted them to have power.

The fruit of salvation is **peace**.

The fruit of Pentecost is **power**.

Passover is about receiving the forgiveness of sins and the indwelling of the Holy Spirit. Pentecost is about the Spirit coming upon you to empower you for ministry (Acts 1:8). Passover brings you into a relationship with God. Pentecost empowers you to serve God.

The Spirit *in you* enables you to live the Christian life.

The Spirit *upon you* empowers you to reach the world.

The Spirit *in you* makes you a child of God.

The Spirit *upon you* empowers you to represent Him as a child of God.

The Spirit *in you* brings freedom to you (2 Corinthians 3:17).

The Spirit *upon you* brings freedom to others (Luke 4:18).

The Spirit *in you* enables you to reflect the character of Christ.

The Spirit *upon you* enables you to be a witness for Christ.

The Spirit *in you* enables you to reflect the character of Christ.

The Spirit *upon you* enables you to be a witness for Christ.

The anointing *in you* empowers you to be like Jesus. The anointing *upon you* empowers you to make a difference. He lives *in you* for your sake. He comes *upon you* for the sake of others.

Just because you've had the Passover experience doesn't mean you don't need the Pentecost experience. If you're a

Christian, you've already experienced the Feast of Passover, but have you experienced Pentecost?

It's not enough to have peace with God—you need the power to walk out your purpose. The Holy Spirit wasn't given just to comfort you; He was given to empower you.

The Spirit in you is for personal transformation. The Spirit upon you is for Kingdom advancement.

God wants to fill you with the same power the disciples received on the day of Pentecost. He wants you to walk in the boldness, strength, and supernatural ability that comes from being baptized in the Holy Spirit.

Don't settle for just salvation. Jesus paid the price for both peace and power—so why not receive both?

THE BAPTISM IN THE HOLY SPIRIT WASN'T JUST FOR THE EARLY CHURCH—IT'S FOR EVERY GENERATION.

CHAPTER 4

EVERY GENERATION

One thing I love about our church is how many different generations we have represented.

The oldest generation is the **Silent Generation** (born in the late 1920s to mid-1940s). They were called the silent generation because, as children, they were taught to be seen and not heard. This generation valued hard work, loyalty, and respect for authority.

Then you have the **Baby Boomers** (born in the mid-1940s to mid-1960s). This generation perfected smoking. They smoked at home, at work, and even at restaurants—between bites. They smoked with their children in the car...with the windows rolled up.

After Boomers come the **Millennials** (born in the early 1980s to mid-1990s)—and let's be honest, Boomers don't like Millennials. Well, nobody really likes Millennials. I think it's because they invented avocado toast and put pumpkin spice on everything. But honestly, it's not their fault their version of ***Star Wars*** had Jar Jar Binks.

Then there's **Gen Z** (born in the mid-1990s to early 2010s). There is so much that Gen Z doesn't know. They don't know how to read cursive. They don't know how to use a paper map and they can't get anywhere without GPS.

They don't know how to write a check, address an envelope, or mail a letter. I had a Gen Z staff member send a flyer for our youth camp to all the parents in our church. He went to the post office and saw the stamps that were $0.66 and $0.01. He thought the one-cent stamps would be cheaper and proceeded to mail out 250 flyers with one-cent stamps, which, of course, were returned to the church.

I'm just saying that if Gen Z takes over the world, it will be pretty easy to get it back. Write the battle plans in cursive, put them on a piece of paper, and send them in the mail.

Did I forget anyone? Oh yeah—**Gen X** (born in the mid-1960s to early 1980s). That's my generation. I didn't forget Gen X, but they are called the forgotten generation.

CBS once did a segment on the different generations, and they forgot Gen X. All 65 million of us. But the thing is, we don't care. We raised ourselves. We are the latchkey generation. Nobody cared that we were bored. Nobody cared about our grades.

We didn't wear seatbelts—not even in the front seat. If your mom's arm wasn't strong enough, you were going through the windshield.

We didn't have juice boxes or goldfish crackers for snack time. If we were thirsty, we drank out of the garden hose. Our parents didn't arrange playdates. The closest thing we had to a play date was when our parents would tell us to go outside and play and then lock the door behind us.

And dodgeball? Forget those soft foam balls kids use today—we had the real ones. Thick, red, rubber balls that left cross-hatch marks on your face. If you weren't bleeding or seeing stars, you were fine.

What happened in Acts 2 became the model for believers in the church.

We didn't have helicopter parents. We had the opposite of helicopter parents. When we got hurt, we were told to quit crying, rub some dirt on it, and walk it off.

Each generation is unique because each one lived through different events and shared distinct experiences that shaped the individuals during that period of time.

Many Christians today believe that what happened on the day of Pentecost was just for that generation. They see it as a one-time event—a unique experience for the believers in Acts 2 to mark the beginning of the church. But that's not what Scripture teaches.

A PROMISE FOR EVERY GENERATION

On the day of Pentecost, after the Holy Spirit was poured out, there was quite a commotion in the city. People gathered in Jerusalem for the Feast of Pentecost were wondering what had just happened in the upper room.

Peter stood up and addressed the crowd, explaining that what they were witnessing was the fulfillment of the prophecy from Joel 2:28–32—that God would pour out His Spirit on all people. Peter proclaimed the Gospel and finished by saying this:

> "Repent, and let every one of you be baptized in the name of Jesus Christ for the remission of sins; and you shall receive the gift of the Holy Spirit. For the promise is to *you* and to *your children*, and to *all who are afar off, as many as the Lord our God will call*."
>
> ACTS 2:38-39 NKJV (EMPHASIS ADDED)

Whenever Scripture mentions the phrase "the gift of the Holy Spirit," "the promise of the Father," or "baptism in the Holy Spirit," it's talking about the same thing. These terms are used interchangeably throughout the New Testament.

Notice Peter didn't say this gift was just for the apostles or just for the believers in the upper room. He said it was for:

You – the people standing in front of him that day.

Your children – the next generation.

All who are afar off – future generations, including us.

As many as the Lord our God will call – in other words, all believers for all time.

This experience wasn't just for the early church—it's for every generation. That's why we see this same pattern repeated throughout the book of Acts. Over and over again, people were saved, baptized in water, and then baptized in the Holy Spirit. What happened in Acts 2 didn't stop there—it became the model for believers in the church.

ACTS 8

In Acts 8, about a year after the events of Acts 2, Philip went to Samaria and preached the Gospel. Many people believed, gave their lives to Christ, and were baptized in water.

When the apostles in Jerusalem heard that Samaria had accepted the word of God, they sent Peter and John to Samaria. When they arrived, they prayed for the new believers there that they might receive the Holy Spirit, because the Holy Spirit had not yet come upon any of them; they had simply been baptized in the name of the Lord Jesus. Then Peter and John placed their hands on them, and they received the Holy Spirit.

ACTS 8:14-17 NKJV

These people received the Word of God, gave their lives to Christ, and were baptized in water, which means the Holy Spirit was in them, but it says the Holy Spirit had not yet come upon them.

So they sent for the Apostles who prayed for them that they might receive the Holy Spirit. Now, obviously, this is not talking about receiving the Holy Spirit at salvation. When you give your life to Christ, the Holy Spirit comes to live inside of you.

If anyone does not have the Spirit of Christ, they do not belong to Christ,

ROMANS 8:9 NIV

If you don't have the Holy Spirit in you, then you're not a Christian because, at the moment of salvation, the Holy Spirit comes to live inside of you (1 Corinthians 3:16).

This clearly refers to another experience with the Holy Spirit that is subsequent to receiving the Holy Spirit at salvation, which is described as the Holy Spirit coming upon someone. This language is consistent with how Scripture describes the baptism in the Holy Spirit—it's an experience where the Spirit comes upon you, distinct from the Spirit dwelling within you at salvation.

The Holy Spirit lives in you at salvation, but He comes upon you when you are baptized in the Holy Spirit. In fact, from Acts 2 onward, whenever it mentions someone receiving the Holy Spirit, it's referring to the baptism in the Holy Spirit, not receiving the Spirit at salvation.

So the apostles came and laid their hands on them, and they received the Holy Spirit. Once again, we know this is a separate and distinct experience from receiving the Holy Spirit at salvation because no one believes that you have to have someone lay hands on you for you to receive the Holy Spirit at salvation.

It is a work of the Spirit that happens the instant you are saved. However, laying hands on someone to pray for the Holy Spirit to come upon them is one of the ways someone receives the baptism in the Holy Spirit (Acts 9:17-18; Acts 19:1-6)

As you can see, the baptism in the Holy Spirit is a separate experience from receiving the Holy Spirit at salvation. What happened in Acts 2 is repeated here in Acts 8, a full year after Pentecost.

ACTS 9

In Acts 9, the early church experienced intense persecution at the hands of Saul (who would later become the apostle Paul). Saul went from house to house, dragging Christians out of their homes and throwing them into prison. He even approved of the stoning of Stephen, the first Christian martyr.

However, when Saul was on his way to Damascus, he had an encounter with Jesus that changed everything. There, he confessed Jesus as Lord (Acts 9:4-6). Now, if you believe Jesus rose from the grave and you confess Him as Lord, you are saved (Romans 10:9-10).

At this moment, Saul experienced salvation, but this encounter leaves him physically blind. Jesus told him where to go and where he would receive instructions on what to do next.

Saul waited at this home for three days.

And Ananias went his way and entered the house; and laying his hands on him he said, 'Brother Saul, the Lord Jesus, who appeared to you on the road as you came, has sent me that you may receive your sight and be filled with the Holy Spirit.' Immediately something like scales fell from Saul's eyes, and he could see again. He got up and was baptized.

ACTS 9:17-18 NIV

Here, Saul was saved for three days, then filled with the Spirit (another term for the baptism in the Holy Spirit according to Acts 2:1-4), and then water baptized. Once again, we see a separate experience with the Holy Spirit that is subsequent to receiving the Holy Spirit at salvation. This follows the same pattern we've already seen:

Saul was **saved**.

He was **baptized** in the Holy Spirit.

Then he was **baptized in water**.

What happened in Acts 2 and Acts 8 is repeated here in Acts 9—confirming that the baptism in the Holy Spirit is a separate experience from salvation. Saul's experience reinforces the pattern that salvation, water baptism and Spirit baptism are distinct encounters available to every believer.

ACTS 10

Acts 10 marks a pivotal moment in the early church. Up until this point, the Gospel had only been preached to Jews and Samaritans. But now, God was about to break down that barrier and extend salvation to the Gentiles.

Cornelius, a Roman centurion and devout Gentile, had a vision where an angel told him to send for the Apostle Peter. Meanwhile, Peter had a vision of his own where God showed him that what was once considered unclean was now clean—symbolizing the removal of barriers between Jews and Gentiles. Peter goes to Cornelius' house and preaches the Gospel.

> While Peter was still speaking these words, the Holy Spirit fell upon all those who heard the word. And those of the circumcision who believed were astonished, as many as came with Peter, because the gift of the Holy Spirit had been poured out on the Gentiles also. For they heard them speak with tongues and magnify God. Then Peter answered, "Can anyone forbid water, that these should not be baptized who have received the Holy Spirit just as we have?" And he commanded them to be baptized in the name of the Lord.
>
> ACTS 10:44-48 NKJV

While Peter preached, they were baptized in the Holy Spirit and spoke in tongues. Peter says, "They received the Holy Spirit just as we have." The same thing that happened on Pentecost happened again in Acts chapter 10.

Luke uses the word *fell* to describe what happened:

> The Holy Spirit fell upon those who heard the word.
>
> ACTS 10:44 NKJV

The Greek word for *fell* here is *epipiptō*,[1] which means *to press upon, to rush upon, to embrace.* It's the same word used in Mark 3:10 to describe sick people pressing in to touch Jesus. It's the same word used when Paul fell on the young boy who died after falling from a window and raised him back to life (Acts 20:10). And it's the same word used in the story of the prodigal son, when the father saw his son and "*fell on his neck* and kissed him" (Luke 15:20).

As you can see, this word means to press upon, to grip, to hug, and to embrace, and here in Acts 10:44, it's used to describe the baptism in the Holy Spirit. This isn't receiving the indwelling of the Holy Spirit; it's the Holy Spirit coming *upon you, pressing upon you,* and *embracing you.* The language itself speaks of a separate experience.

Drinking water is vital to your health and well-being. When you drink water, the water is *in* you, but it's not *upon* you. For the water to be upon you, the water would need to be poured over your head.

Drinking water is essential for life, and having the Holy Spirit *in* you is essential for eternal life. Without the indwelling Spirit, you are not saved, so getting water in you is the most important thing. But on a hot summer day, there is nothing like pouring water over you to cool and refresh you.

The baptism in the Holy Spirit isn't when you receive the Holy Spirit on the inside; it's when the Spirit comes *upon* you. Jesus used the analogy of water to describe these two experiences with the Holy Spirit.

> Jesus answered, "Everyone who drinks this water will be thirsty again, but whoever drinks the water I give them will never thirst. Indeed, the water I give them will become in them a spring of water welling up to eternal life."
>
> JOHN 4:13-14 NIV

In this passage, Jesus speaks to the Samaritan woman at the well and uses the metaphor of water to describe the Holy Spirit, who would become a source of spiritual life within believers.

When you put trust in Jesus, you drink the living water that becomes in you a well, springing up to eternal life. However, in John 7, Jesus describes a different experience with the Holy Spirit.

> On the last and most important day of the festival, Jesus stood up and shouted, "All who are thirsty should come to me! All who believe in me should drink! As the scriptures said concerning me, Rivers of living water will flow out from within him."
>
> JOHN 7:37-39 CEB

Jesus said this concerning the Spirit. Those who believed in him would soon receive the Spirit, but they hadn't experienced the Spirit yet since Jesus hadn't yet been glorified.

Out of the exalted, glorified Christ will flow rivers of living water. The Holy Spirit will pour out of the ascended Christ like a river. There is a difference between having a well inside of you and being caught up in the river of the Holy Spirit.

The well is inside of you at salvation, but the river flows to you and comes *upon* you when you are baptized in the Holy Spirit.

IT'S POSSIBLE TO RECEIVE THE HOLY SPIRIT AT SALVATION AND STILL NOT EXPERIENCE THE BAPTISM IN THE HOLY SPIRIT.

CHAPTER 5

DID YOU RECEIVE?

Have you ever tried putting together a basketball hoop? Not the little ones for kids—the full-size driveway goal with a glass backboard, adjustable height, and a 70-pound base.

It always seems simple at first. You look at the picture on the box and think, *"This'll be a fun project."* But six hours later, you're sweating, sunburned, and re-reading step 17 for the fourth time—wondering why the rim still wobbles and where those three extra bolts were supposed to go.

It looks done. It mostly works. But something's off.

That's exactly what happened in Acts 19. Paul came across a group of disciples in Ephesus but when Paul talked to them, he realized something wasn't quite right. So he asked one simple question:

"Did you receive the Holy Spirit when you believed?"

If you received everything at salvation, Paul wouldn't need to ask if they received the Holy Spirit when they believed. Paul's question tells us something important: not everything happens at salvation. Paul wasn't talking about receiving the Holy Spirit at salvation. This is the same Paul who wrote in Romans 8:9, *"And if anyone does not have the Spirit of Christ, they do not belong to Christ."* He knew that the Spirit lives in believers at salvation. But he was asking about something more—a second experience with the Holy Spirit.

This means it's possible to receive the Holy Spirit at salvation and *still not* experience the baptism in the Holy Spirit. Some say, "You get everything the moment you are saved." Well, the greatest apostle to ever live didn't believe that because he asked if they received the Holy Spirit after they believed.

> **If people don't hear the baptism in the Holy Spirit being preached, they will not receive it.**

On top of that, Jesus told us to *ask* for the Holy Spirit (Luke 11:13). Why would Jesus tell us to ask for the Holy Spirit if it's something you automatically receive when you're saved? Why would Paul ask a group of disciples if they had received the Spirit after they believed? Because there is a second experience with the Holy Spirit after salvation that isn't automatic. You must ask for it and receive it.

Notice the emphasis that Paul placed on baptism in the Holy Spirit. It was the first question he asked when encountering a group of disciples. This was a high priority in the early church.

Today, when you get saved, the church gives you a pamphlet, bakes you an apple pie, and tells you to get plugged into a small group. You could sit in that church for 30 years and never hear about the baptism in the Holy Spirit.

But this was the top priority in the early church. It wasn't seen as an optional add-on; it was Paul's first concern when he encountered new believers. He wanted to make sure they were empowered by the Holy Spirit.

> And it happened, while Apollos was at Corinth, that Paul, having passed through the upper regions, came to Ephesus. And finding some disciples he said to them, "Did you receive the Holy Spirit when you believed?" So they said to him, "We have not so much as heard whether there is a Holy Spirit."
>
> ACTS 19:1-2 NKJV

People will not receive what they don't hear preached to them. I've heard pastors say, "I'm filled with the Holy Spirit. Most of our staff is also, but I don't discuss it on Sunday because people think it's weird."

That's wrong. That's like knowing where free food is and refusing to tell hungry people where to get it. If people don't hear the baptism in the Holy Spirit being preached, they will not receive it.

> And he said to them, "Into what then were you baptized?" So they said, "Into John's baptism."Then Paul said, "John indeed baptized with a baptism of repentance, saying to the people that they should believe on Him who would come after him, that is, on Christ Jesus."When they heard this, they were baptized in the name of the Lord Jesus.
>
> ACTS 19:3-5 NKJV

Some say, "We haven't even heard of the Holy Spirit." Apparently, they were Baptists. They were literally Baptists—disciples of John the Baptist! So Paul tells them about Jesus, they get saved, and then they are baptized in water.

> And when Paul had laid hands on them, the Holy Spirit came upon them, and they spoke with tongues and prophesied.
>
> ACTS 19:6 NKJV

Again, this is a clear example of the three baptisms: They believed in Jesus and were baptized into Christ (salvation). They were baptized in water. Then they received the baptism in the Holy Spirit.

Over and over again, we see people giving their lives to Jesus, being baptized in water, and then the Holy Spirit coming upon them. It happened in Jerusalem, it happened in Samaria, and it happened in Ephesus.

THE PATTERN

Some people say, "There is only one experience with the Holy Spirit that happens at salvation. After the initial infilling of the Holy Spirit, there is nothing else to receive." However, that's not what happened in Jerusalem, Samaria, or Ephesus. They all had a second experience of being baptized in the Holy Spirit after salvation, showing that the baptism in the Holy Spirit is subsequent to receiving the Holy Spirit at salvation.

> **The Book of Acts isn't just a history book—it's a pattern book.**

Some say the baptism in the Holy Spirit was a special experience for the first couple of years of the church to help it grow and get off the ground, but that's not what the Bible teaches. This was God's pattern for working with believers all through the Book of Acts.

Let's do a quick timeline check:

The Holy Spirit was poured out on the Day of Pentecost in **AD 30**.

Philip went to Samaria in **AD 31** and new believers were baptized in the Holy Spirit.

Paul was baptized in the Holy Spirit in **AD 34** (Acts 9).

Cornelius' house was saved and baptized in the Holy Spirit in **AD 37** (Acts 10).

The account in Ephesus (Acts 19) happened in **AD 53**—a full 23 years after Pentecost.

This shows that the baptism in the Holy Spirit wasn't a one-time event or an added bonus to help get the early church up and running. It was God's pattern for working with believers throughout the church age.

The Book of Acts isn't just a history book—it's a pattern book. It's a blueprint of how God works in and through His church. And we are part of that same church. The book of Acts takes place in the church age—which we are still in.

The Gospel hasn't changed. Jesus' name hasn't changed. The Holy Spirit hasn't changed.

We are part of the same church as the Book of Acts. That means the same experience they had with the Holy Spirit is available to believers today.

HAVE YOU RECEIVED THE HOLY SPIRIT?

So let me ask you the same question the apostle Paul asked the disciples in Ephesus: Have you received the Holy Spirit since you believed?

Dr. Peter Lord pastored Park Avenue Church for 30 years in Titusville, Florida. He was preaching a series on the Holy Spirit, but he was trained through his theological upbringing that the baptism of the Holy Spirit was not for today.

As he was studying for the series, the Lord spoke to him and said, "Have you received the Holy Spirit?"

He said, "Of course, Lord. The Holy Spirit lives in me. The Holy Spirit came into my life the moment I received Christ. Of course, I received Him."

At that time, his mother-in-law had come to live with them, and they didn't exactly agree on everything. The Lord said, "Your mother-in-law lives in your house, but have you received her?"

He said, "Not fully..."

And the Lord said, "The Holy Spirit lives in your house, but because of your upbringing, you have not fully received Him either."

Many people, because of their theological upbringing, haven't fully received the Holy Spirit. They've received the indwelling of the Holy Spirit at salvation, but they haven't been baptized in the Holy Spirit. They haven't received the fullness of the Spirit's power in their lives—which is essential for every believer.

God wants to fill you with His Spirit, empower you for ministry, and equip you to fulfill His calling on your life.

The question is: **Are you ready to receive it?**

THE PROMISE OF THE HOLY SPIRIT GIVES US THE POWER WE NEED TO DO WHAT WE CANNOT DO ON OUR OWN.

CHAPTER 6

POWER

A couple of years ago, we took our kids on vacation to Disney World - the happiest place on earth. You know, that place you go and spend an insane amount of money to stand in line all day in the blazing heat and convince yourself you're in the happiest place on earth and not purgatory.

I love what Comedian Jim Gaffigan said about Disney. He said, "If you haven't been to Disney World, it's like the DMV for kids. Just imagine standing in line at the DMV, only it's in Orlando in the summer, so imagine you are standing in line on the surface of the sun."

The real magic of Disney is that you can carry around screaming children for 14 hours a day, sweating through your shirt in 100-degree weather with 100% humidity, and still gain weight. That is the real magic of Disney.

After taking my kids to Disney, I finally understood why my dad was always in a bad mood on vacation. He spent an enormous amount of money to be uncomfortable, sweaty, and sticky while listening to us whine and complain about everything.

The worst part of Disney World is the lines. After being in the park for 6 hours, we only went on three rides. I stood in line for the Dumbo ride for an hour and a half. After that ride, I felt like a Dumbo for standing in that line.

I didn't like many of the rides, but there was one that was amazing. I look forward to this ride every single day; it's the air-conditioned bus ride back to the hotel. It's the best ride at Disney.

I think Disney World would be the happiest place on earth if you didn't have to wait in line all day. There is nothing worse than waiting. I like it when things move. When they are quick. My favorite word is "go," not "wait."

I love that when Jesus rose from the dead and appeared to His disciples, He told them to go out into all the world and preach the Gospel. This command is called the Great Commission.

And Jesus came and spoke to them, saying, "All authority has been given to Me in heaven and on earth. Go therefore and make disciples of all the nations, baptizing them in the name of the Father and of the Son and of the Holy Spirit, teaching them to observe all things that I have commanded you; and lo, I am with you always, even to the end of the age." Amen.

MATTHEW 28:18-20 NKJV

This sounds like Jesus' final words before he ascends to heaven—especially with the "Amen" at the end. However, these were not Jesus' last words. Jesus' final instruction to His disciples is found in the first chapter of Acts.

And being assembled together with them, He commanded them not to depart from Jerusalem, but to wait for the Promise of the Father, "which," He said, "you have heard from Me; for John truly baptized with water, but you shall be baptized with the Holy Spirit not many days from now."

ACTS 1:4-5 NKJV

The disciples are ready to tell the world that Jesus is alive, but before Jesus tells them to go, He tells them to wait. We live in a "go" culture. Move fast. Do more. Don't wait. So it's no surprise that we love the Great Commission. "Go into all the world!" Feels right. Feels urgent. But Jesus didn't end His earthly ministry with "Go." His final word to the disciples wasn't "Go"—it was "Wait."

What were they to wait for? The Promise of the Father. Receiving The Promise was so important that Jesus told his disciples not to go into the world and preach the Gospel until after they were immersed in the Spirit.

Why? God knew that without the empowerment of the Spirit, they would not be able to fulfill the Great Commission. Without The Promise, they would only have their natural ability, which wasn't enough.

"I am going to send you what my Father has promised; but stay in the city until you have been clothed with power from on high."
LUKE 24:49 NIV

The promise of the Holy Spirit gives us the power we need to do what we cannot do on our own. God never intended for us to handle the pressures of life on our own—He intended for us to have **power.**

The Greek word for power is *dunamis*[1]—meaning miraculous strength, divine ability, and moral excellence. The baptism in the Holy Spirit gives us access to this supernatural strength.

Knowing what to do isn't the problem. It's doing it that's hard. We need more than principles—we need power.

Think about the disciples. For three and a half years, they sat at Jesus' feet, learning directly from Him. You would think that after spending that much time with Him, they'd have everything they needed to be victorious. But when it comes to living the Christian life, information alone isn't enough—we need supernatural power.

God's principles are impossible without God's power:

Love your enemies (Matthew 5:44).

Bless those who curse you (Luke 6:28).

Forgive those who sin against you (Matthew 6:14-15).

Honor your father and mother (Ephesians 6:2-3).

Bear one another's burdens (Galatians 6:2).

Deny yourself and take up your cross (Luke 9:23).

Without the power of the Holy Spirit, these commands aren't just difficult—they're impossible. That's why the last command Jesus gave His disciples was to stay in Jerusalem until they received the power of the Holy Spirit (Acts 1:8).

ESSENTIAL

When my wife and I had our first baby, our friends threw a baby shower for us. We received every kind of baby product, gadget, and item you could imagine: a crib, swaddling blankets, bumper pads, a baby swing, a bouncer, a Bumbo seat, a baby bath, a baby bath thermometer, bottles, a bottle warmer, tummy time mats, a baby food maker, pacifiers, pacifier wipes, changing pads, a changing basket, wipe warmers, diaper pails—and even a snot sucker.

We had a white noise machine that was supposed to simulate the sound a baby hears in the womb. It's supposed to calm the baby and help them sleep. My wife pressed play, and I said, "What is that?" She answered, "That's the sound the baby heard in my tummy." I said, "Did you eat a radio that wasn't dialed into the right station?"

We had this baby wrap. It's just a long cloth that you wrap around yourself in 37 different ways, then jam a baby in there who will sleep forever in that thing.

Me doing that wrap is the same thing as when ladies get out of the shower and wrap their hair up in a towel as a monument to soft-serve ice cream. We had everything you could think of; we even had baby shoes, and babies don't walk.

We got all these things that we thought were essential to raising a child, but it turns out we didn't need 90% of those things. By the time we had our second child, it was a completely different story.

He took a bath in the sink. Drank a cold bottle. Ate baby food from the store. His tummy time mat was the rug in the living room. We changed his diaper on the floor and wiped his butt with cold wipes. When he dropped his pacifier on the ground, it didn't get cleaned with a specialty disinfectant wipe. I just brushed off the dirt and stuck it back in his mouth.

There were so many things we thought we had to have for our first baby but it turns out they were optional, not essential. The baptism in the Holy Spirit is nothing like all the baby merch found in stores today. It's not an optional accessory that may come in handy. It's essential for doing what God has called you to do.

PETER'S TRANSFORMATION

Peter is the perfect example of why we need the power of the Holy Spirit. He always seemed to get it wrong.

One time, Jesus asked His disciples, "Who do the people say that I am?" Peter said, "You are the Christ, the Son of the living God." Jesus replied, "Good job, Peter."

Then Jesus told the disciples that He would have to suffer and die—and Peter **rebuked Jesus!**

You know you're on the wrong side of an issue when you find yourself rebuking Jesus.

When Jesus was getting arrested, Peter was the one who took out a sword and cut off a man's ear, and Jesus had to put it back on. Peter is seen all throughout the Gospels saying and doing the wrong thing at the wrong time.

But Peter's biggest mistake was denying Christ. The night before Jesus was betrayed, Jesus told his disciples what would happen and how they would all fall away.

> Peter declared, "Even if everyone else deserts you, I will never desert you." Jesus replied, "I tell you the truth, Peter—this very night, before the rooster crows, you will deny three times that you even know me."
>
> MATTHEW 26:33-34 NLT

Peter didn't want to fall away. He wanted to stand up for Christ. He said, "I will die before I deny you," but then later on that night, he denied Jesus three times. He didn't even have the courage to stand up to a young girl who asked if he was a disciple of Jesus.

Peter wanted to stand for Christ in the face of adversity. He wanted to do the right thing; he just didn't have the power. But in Acts 2, after the Holy Spirit came upon the disciples in the upper room, Peter stood up and boldly proclaimed the Gospel.

In Acts 4, Peter stood before the same Sanhedrin that had condemned Jesus and said:

> "Jesus Christ the Nazarene, the man you crucified but whom God raised from the dead...There is salvation in no one else! God has given no other name under heaven by which we must be saved."
>
> ACTS 4:10-12 NLT

Then the Sanhedrin commanded them not to speak or teach in the name of Jesus, and Peter answered and said,

> "Do you think God wants us to obey you rather than Him? We cannot stop telling everything we have seen and heard."
>
> ACTS 4:19-20 NLT

This is the same Peter who denied knowing Jesus, now boldly proclaiming Jesus and even defying the Sanhedrin. What is responsible for this sudden change in Peter's life? **The baptism of the Holy Spirit** (Acts 4:8).

It gave him the power and boldness to stand for Christ when he previously had failed in his own strength. The same Holy Spirit who transformed Peter's life is still empowering believers today. The Holy Spirit empowers us to experience victory in every area where we have failed in our own strength.

D.L. MOODY

D.L. Moody was an American evangelist in the late 1800s who founded Moody Church and Moody Bible Institute. During his life, he preached the Gospel to 100 million people and was a prominent figure in the second great awakening in America. Many claim he was the greatest evangelist of the 19th century.

How did a shoe salesman who didn't complete elementary school change a nation? The baptism in the Holy Spirit. D.L. Moody started a Sunday school class that grew into a church. His ministry experienced moderate success but nothing extraordinary.

Everything changed when two women from his church approached him after a service. They told him, *"We've been praying for you."*

Moody responded, *"Why don't you pray for the people?"*

They answered, *"Because you need power."*

Moody thought he had power, but his conversation with those two women caused him to pray for the power of the Holy Spirit like never before.

Moody said,

> *"I really felt that I did not want to live if I could not have this power for service. The hunger increased. I was praying all the time that God would fill me with His Holy Spirit. Well, one day in the city of New York—oh, what a day! I cannot describe it. I had such an experience of His love that I asked Him to stay His hand.*
>
> *I went to preaching again. The sermons were not different—I didn't present any new truths—and yet hundreds were converted."*[2]

Moody's sermons didn't change. His ministry techniques didn't change. What changed? The power of the Holy Spirit.

When you're baptized in the Spirit, you'll go back to doing the same thing you were doing before, only you'll get different results. Whether you're a pastor, businessman, teacher, construction worker, or farmer, you'll do the same thing you did before, but the results will be different because of the power of the Holy Spirit.

THE ANOINTING

You need the anointing of the Holy Spirit to do what God has called you to do.

I need the anointing to pastor. Why? Because there are people involved—and some of them are crazy. If you haven't met any crazy Christians, that's a bad sign. It probably means *you're* the crazy one.

Without the Holy Spirit, I'm a below-average pastor and preacher. I need the anointing of the Holy Spirit on my life to do what God has called me to do.

But the anointing isn't just for pastors and preachers—it's for **everyone**. It's for whatever God has called you to do.

It's important to understand that the anointing isn't just to help pastors to preach; it's to help entrepreneurs start new businesses; it's to help designers create; it's to help authors to write; it's to help educators teach.

The anointing is for everyone in whatever sphere of influence you have. The anointing helps us accomplish what we cannot do in our own ability.

The anointing helped Joshua lead.

The anointing gave Samson supernatural strength.

The anointing empowered David to rule as king.

The anointing gave Daniel the ability to interpret dreams.

The anointing strengthened Zerubbabel to rebuild the temple.

In the same way, the Holy Spirit worked and moved in the lives of these individuals; He wants to work and move in your life, empowering you to do what you cannot do on your own.

MY STORY

I gave my life to Christ at the age of seven. I knew Jesus died for me and rose again. But even though I gave my life to Jesus at a young age, I didn't really grow up in church. My family went to church off and on over the years, but it wasn't a consistent part of my life. Still, I remained devoted to Jesus throughout my childhood and into high school.

After high school, I went to a Christian college to play basketball. I didn't choose the school because it was Christian—I was just there to play ball. But because it was a Christian school, we had to take one Bible class every semester.

This particular college was **cessationist**. They believed that the baptism in the Holy Spirit, the gifts of the Spirit, speaking in tongues, miracles, and healing were for the early church—but not for today.

The theological term for this is **cessationism**—the belief that the miraculous gifts of the Holy Spirit ceased after the Apostolic Age.

But my roommate ended up being a Pentecostal preacher who spoke in tongues daily. Even though I didn't grow up in church, I had read the Bible enough to know that the gifts of the Spirit and the power of God are **for today.**

One day, I heard my roommate speaking in tongues and asked him about it. He told me it was a gift you receive when you are baptized in the Holy Spirit. Then he said, *"Do you want to receive it?"*

I said, *"Yes!"*

So we broke into the chapel on campus, and he laid hands on me and prayed for me to receive the Holy Spirit. And don't worry—the Holy Spirit broke in too because He wasn't exactly welcome in that chapel.

Suddenly, I felt the power of God flow through me—like electricity surging in my body. The more I prayed, the stronger the power got.

The power of God was so intense that I could barely stand. I dropped to my knees and began to speak in tongues. The more I prayed in tongues, the stronger God's presence became, so I laid down on the ground, overwhelmed by the power of God.

I thought I had been on the floor for 10 minutes, but when I got up, it had been over an hour.

When I walked outside, everything looked different. The sky was bluer. The grass was greener. I can't fully describe it, but I've talked to other people who had the same experience. It was like my senses had been sharpened.

But the biggest change wasn't what I saw—it was what happened inside of me.

I'm an introvert and before this experience, I was so anxious in social situations that I could barely carry on a conversation with a stranger, let alone speak in front of people.

At this college, we had to attend a weekly prayer group. I had two very sweet elderly women in my group, and when it was my turn to pray, I was so nervous that I couldn't get a word out.

I lived with crippling anxiety every single day.

But when the Holy Spirit came upon me that day, everything changed. I was still an introvert—but I was no longer trapped by fear. Boldness isn't about becoming someone you're not—it's about being free to be exactly who God created you to be.

I had a confidence I never had before. I wasn't afraid to speak in front of others anymore. I could now step into what God had called me to do without the weight of fear holding me back.

There is no way I could do what I do today if I hadn't been baptized in the Holy Spirit.

My life wasn't transformed when I got saved or baptized in water. Those were defining moments—but my life was completely transformed when I was baptized in the Holy Spirit. And that same power is available to you.

LIVING EMPOWERED

God never intended for you to handle life's pressures on your own. He intended for you to walk in **power**. The baptism in the Holy Spirit isn't about securing your place in heaven—it's about living with strength and victory right now.

You need the power of the Holy Spirit to get on social media without losing your mind.

You need the power of the Holy Spirit to navigate your workplace without bitterness.

You need the power of the Holy Spirit to deal with your dysfunctional family.

You need the power of the Holy Spirit to parent your crazy kids.

You need the power of the Holy Spirit to have a healthy marriage.

You need the power of the Holy Spirit to handle the stress and pressure of life without breaking.

Many Christians limit the Holy Spirit to being a counselor, comforter, and helper. He is all those things—but He is also the **power source** of the Christian life. He empowers you to conquer every area where you've consistently failed using your own strength.

Why keep driving in fourth gear when there's a fifth gear available? Why keep climbing the stairs when an escalator is right next to you?

Stop living stuck. Don't settle for fourth gear.

Step into the power that's already yours.

You were made to live **empowered**.

A LOT OF WHAT PEOPLE BELIEVE ABOUT SPEAKING IN TONGUES ISN'T BASED ON TRUTH— IT'S BASED ON TRADITION.

CHAPTER 7

SPEAKING IN TONGUES

I grew up in Las Vegas, Nevada, and moved to South Georgia in my twenties. Right away, I noticed that people talk differently in the South—and it's not just the accent. It's the phrases.

They say things like, "I love him to death, but..." And whenever someone says that—they're about to say something terrible. "I love him to death, but..." is Southern for, *I'm about rip this person apart.*

Same thing with "Bless his heart..." If you hear, "Bless his heart," don't be fooled—it's not a compliment. It's just verbal camouflage for an insult. Add "bless his heart" in front of anything and, for some reason, Southerners think it's sanctified.

Then there are the weird metaphors: "That's as easy as shooting fish in a barrel." Is that easy? I've never shot at a fish in a barrel.

And what's with all the cat sayings? "There's more than one way to skin a cat." Why do you know that? And why are you skinning cats in the first place? "He's like a cat on a hot tin roof." "I'm as busy as a one-legged cat in a sandbox..." Stop torturing cats.

And just when I thought I was catching on—they started making up words. I was playing football with a friend and he yelled, "Chunk it!" I said, "What?" He said, "Chunk it!"
I said, "You mean chuck it. You *chuck* a ball, you don't *chunk* it."

I was riding down the road with a roommate and he cut someone off, and the other driver gave him the international sign for "You're number one." My roommate said, "He flicked me off." I said, "No—he flipped you off. You *flick* a bugger. You *flip* the bird."

Another time one of my friends punched another guy in the arm, left a big red mark, and the guy said, "You gave me a whelp!" No, that's a *welt*, not a *whelp*. A whelp is a baby animal, not a bruise.

What I realized is this: in the South, people's language is often based on tradition—not truth. They say things because that's what they've always heard. That's what they were taught. Their speech isn't shaped by what's right—it's shaped by what tradition.

TRADITION & TRUTH

The same thing happens when it comes to speaking in tongues. A lot of what people believe about it isn't based on truth—it's based on tradition.

Much of what people have learned about speaking in tongues is based on their denominational upbringing and not the truth of God's Word. It's based on what other people say, not what God said.

Some people have been told it's just emotionalism. Others think it's gibberish. I've even heard people say it's from the devil—which makes no sense. How can a gift from God be from the devil? Even if someone was just making it up and saying nonsense, that still wouldn't make it demonic.

Then there are the folks who say, "Well, it was real once—but it passed away when the apostles died." Or, "It's a gift, sure, but only a few special people have it." Others downplay it by saying, "It's the least of all the gifts"—like it's the spiritual participation trophy.

Tongues is a supernatural utterance given by the Holy Spirit that enables a person to speak in an unknown language.

Don't let traditions that have no basis in God's truth talk you out of receiving everything God has for you. Don't let religious tradition keep you from walking in the fullness of what God has for you. I want to help you sort out fact from fiction when it comes to speaking in tongues.

WHAT IS TONGUES?

What exactly is speaking in tongues? The word *tongues*[1] is the Greek word *glōssa*, which means language. Speaking in tongues is when an individual speaks a language that he or she does not know. It is a supernatural utterance given by the Holy Spirit that enables a person to speak in an unknown language (1 Corinthians 14:2).

The language can be an existing human language with which the speaker is unfamiliar (Acts 2:8-11) or a heavenly language that isn't understood by others (1 Corinthians 14:2).

When you speak in tongues, the Holy Spirit imparts a language to your spirit, and you give voice to what the Holy Spirit is speaking through you, but you don't understand what you're saying.

It functions as a form of prayer or praise that transcends human understanding, allowing for direct communication with God.

THE BAPTISM IN THE HOLY SPIRIT & SPEAKING IN TONGUES

This gift is connected to the baptism in the Holy Spirit. Throughout the Book of Acts, people spoke in tongues when the Spirit came upon them.

> And they were all filled with the Holy Spirit and began to speak with other tongues, as the Spirit gave them utterance.
>
> ACTS 2:4 NKJV

The Law of First Mention is a principle used in biblical interpretation that emphasizes the significance of the first time a particular word or concept appears in Scripture. The initial occurrence of a term or idea often establishes its fundamental meaning and sets the tone for its subsequent usage throughout the Bible.

On the day of Pentecost, everyone in the upper room spoke in tongues as they were baptized in the Spirit. The first time the baptism in the Holy Spirit is mentioned, it is connected with everyone speaking in tongues.

The Holy Spirit imparts a language to your spirit, and you give voice to what the Holy Spirit is speaking.

Notice this wasn't a gift that a select few received or just for those who were graced with this particular gift. If that were so, then it would have said, "Those who had the gift of tongues spoke as the spirit gave them utterance." But that's not what Scripture says; it says, "They *all* spoke in tongues."

Whatever God initiates for the first time reveals His intention every time. When God baptized everyone in the Holy Spirit, and they all spoke in tongues, it showed that God wants everyone to be filled with the Spirit and speak in tongues.

This is why we see the same thing happen repeatedly throughout the Book of Acts. In Acts chapter 10, Peter goes to Cornelius' house and preaches the Gospel.

> While Peter was still speaking these words, the Holy Spirit fell upon all those who heard the word. Those who came with Peter were astonished because the gift of the Holy Spirit had been poured out on the Gentiles also. For they heard them speak with tongues and magnify God.
>
> ACTS 10:44-46 NKJV

Peter and those with him knew that they had been baptized in the Holy Spirit because they heard them speak in tongues. In

Acts 19, Paul found a group of disciples in Ephesus who hadn't been baptized in the Holy Spirit.

> And when Paul had laid hands on them, the Holy Spirit came upon them, and they spoke with tongues and prophesied.
> ACTS 19:6 NKJV

Some people say, "Well, speaking in tongues is only for preaching the Gospel to the unsaved in their own language, like what happened on Pentecost." Well, if that's true, then who were these people evangelizing? The only other person there was Paul. Tongues aren't just for reaching the lost—they're for your relationship with God.

Almost every time Scripture mentions someone being baptized in the Holy Spirit, it specifically mentions them speaking in tongues. There are only two instances where speaking in tongues is not directly mentioned.

In Acts 8, when Philip went to Samaria and preached the Gospel, many people gave their lives to Christ and were baptized in water. Then Peter and John came and laid hands on them to be baptized in the Holy Spirit.

Acts 8 doesn't directly state that they spoke in tongues, but there was some kind of outward demonstration that they had been immersed in the Spirit because Simon the sorcerer saw that the Holy Spirit was given when the apostles laid hands on the people.

He offered them money for the power to lay hands on people to receive the Holy Spirit. Peter rebuked him for thinking he could buy this gift.

> But Peter said to him, "Your money perish with you, because you thought that the gift of God could be purchased with money! You have neither part nor portion in this matter, for your heart is not right in the sight of God."
>
> ACTS 8:20-21

The word *matter*[2] used in this verse is the Greek word *logos*, which means "a word, the act of speaking, speech." This could be translated as, "You have neither part nor portion in this speech." It's possible that Peter was referring to speaking in tongues.

The other instance where tongues are not directly mentioned was when Ananias laid hands on Saul (Paul), and he was filled with the Spirit (Acts 9:17-18). It doesn't specifically mention Paul speaking in tongues here in Acts 9, but we know Paul spoke in tongues because when he wrote to the Corinthians, he said, "I speak in tongues more than all of you" (1 Corinthians 14:18).

PART OF THE PACKAGE

Almost every time Scripture mentions someone being baptized in the Holy Spirit, it specifically mentions them speaking in tongues, and where it is not directly stated, it is implied by other passages.

This connection has caused many to say that the initial physical evidence of receiving the baptism of the Holy Spirit is speaking in tongues.

I don't like the phrase "initial physical evidence." I prefer to say it's part of the package of the baptism in the Holy Spirit. When you order a combo meal at Chick-fil-A, it's going to come with fries and a drink. It's part of the combo meal. Part of the package being baptized in the Holy Spirit is speaking in tongues.

When you buy a pair of shoes, you don't need to say, "I'd like these shoes with the tongues." The tongues come with the shoes. When you bought the shoes, the tongues came with them. You didn't have to ask for the tongues. They came with the shoes.

The baptism in the Spirit is like a good pair of shoes. You ask to be filled with the Spirit, and tongues come with it.

Speaking in tongues is not evidence of being baptized in the Spirit; it's a benefit of being baptized in the Spirit. When you are immersed in the Holy Spirit, you receive the ability to speak in tongues.

This is not a gift that is only reserved for some; it's something everyone receives when they are filled with Spirit.

I went to a ministry school that focused on speaking in tongues as proof you were baptized in the Holy Spirit. So, the entire focus of the Holy Spirit coming upon you was speaking in tongues.

The Scriptures emphasize tongues as a provision of being baptized in the Spirit, not the proof. The ability to speak in tongues is provided for you the moment you are immersed in the Spirit. So, if you don't speak in tongues at the exact moment the Holy Spirit comes upon you, it doesn't mean that you didn't receive the Holy Spirit.

I've prayed for multitudes to be baptized in the Holy Spirit. Many of them speak in tongues the moment we pray for them. For others, they spoke in tongues in the car on the way home or the next morning during their prayer time. For some, it was weeks later. It doesn't mean that they didn't receive the Holy Spirit when they prayed for it because it didn't happen in that instant.

In order to pray in tongues, you have to yield your tongue to the Spirit and speak. Some don't yield their tongue. Some people get in their own way and overthink it. Some refuse to speak, thinking the Holy Spirit will do it all.

For whatever reason, they don't speak in tongues the moment they are baptized in the Holy Spirit. They assume they didn't receive the Holy Spirit because they didn't speak in tongues.

Instead of looking at tongues as the initial evidence of baptism in the Holy Spirit, think of it as the inevitable evidence of being filled with the Spirit. If you prayed to receive the Spirit and didn't speak in tongues, don't worry—you will. As you get a better understanding of this gift and how it operates, you will step out in faith and speak in tongues.

Speaking in tongues is not the goal of baptism in the Holy Spirit. It is the gateway to a Spirit-empowered life. Some people say, "Do I have to speak in tongues?" You don't have to; you get to. Speaking in tongues is not a burden; it's a blessing.

Now, you can live your whole life as a Christian and not pray in tongues, but why would you settle for anything less than everything that God has for you? I don't know about you, but I want everything God has for me. I refuse to settle for anything less than God's best.

THE WORD & THE SPIRIT

Some people say, "Well, I'm not really into the whole speaking in tongues thing. I'm more of a Word person. I don't need to speak in tongues; I just need the Word of God." Well, if you truly are a Word person, you'll have your Bible with you, so grab your Bible and turn to the first page of the Bible, the Table of Contents.

That's right. Put this book aside, open your Bible, and turn to the Table of Contents, and look at the books of the New Testament. First, we have the book of Matthew, written by the apostle Matthew. Matthew was in the upper room on the day of Pentecost, which means he spoke in tongues.

Then we have Mark. Scholars believe Mark was in the upper room because it was his mom's house. Plus, Mark wrote that one of the signs that will follow believers is that they will speak in tongues (Mark 16:17).

Next, we have Luke. Luke is also the author of the book of Acts, so there is a good chance he was in the upper room in Acts 2, which means he would have spoken in tongues.

Then we have the book of John, written by John, the disciple whom Jesus loved (John 13:33). He was in the upper room in Acts 2, so he spoke in tongues. He also wrote 1st John, 2nd John, 3rd John, and Revelation.

The Apostle Paul authored 13 books in the New Testament, including Romans, 1 and 2 Corinthians, Galatians, Ephesians, Philippians, Colossians, 1 and 2 Thessalonians, 1 and 2 Timothy, Titus, and Philemon. Some scholars even believe he wrote the book of Hebrews (we don't know for sure but the illustration works better if he did).

Paul wasn't in the upper room in Acts 2, but we know Paul spoke in tongues because he said, "I speak in tongues more than all of you" (1 Corinthians 14:18).

Then we have the book of James written by James, the half-brother of Jesus. He was in the upper room on the day of Pentecost (Acts 1:14), which means he spoke in tongues.

Then you have 1st and 2nd Peter, written by the apostle Peter, who was the spokesman for what happened on Pentecost, so we know that he spoke in tongues. Lastly, we have the book of Jude.

The Bible does not explicitly state that Jude was in the upper room on the Day of Pentecost. However, Jude is traditionally considered to be one of Jesus' half-brothers. Acts 1:14 mentions that Jesus' brothers were present in the upper room with the apostles and other disciples, so it is possible that he was present for the events in Acts 2.

The Scriptures emphasize tongues as a provision of being baptized in the Spirit, not the proof.

But even if he wasn't, we know Jude spoke in tongues because he wrote in his book, "But you, beloved, building yourselves up on your most holy faith, praying in the Holy Spirit" (Jude 1:20).

You might say, "Well, I'm Catholic. so I pray to Mary." Okay, Mary, the mother of Jesus, spoke in tongues. She was in the upper room on the day of Pentecost. All the New Testament authors and Mary spoke in tongues.

Of course, we know that the Holy Spirit inspired the Word of God (2 Timothy 3:16), but He used people to put pen to paper. Every author in the New Testament (that we know of) spoke in tongues. Since these Spirit-empowered individuals were chosen by God to write His Word, their experience with speaking in tongues validates its authenticity and biblical foundation.

Speaking in tongues doesn't put you at odds with the Word of God. It aligns with the authors of the New Testament and the clear teaching of scripture. It is a natural expression of the Spirit's work in the lives of believers that is consistent with biblical teaching and should not be viewed as suspicious or contrary to God's Word.

Some denominations and churches today are apprehensive of tongues at best. Some think it's in the Bible but unnecessary. Others think it's nothing more than emotionalism. While some believe it's completely unbiblical.

However, speaking in tongues is not out of step with God's Word. It might seem out of step with certain churches today, but it wasn't strange or inconsistent with the early church.

All the early churches spoke in tongues. The church in Jerusalem was a tongue-talking church. The church in Samaria spoke in tongues. The church in Ephesus started with a group of disciples getting filled with the Spirit and speaking in tongues. We know for certain the church in Corinth spoke in tongues. They spoke in tongues so much that the apostle Paul had to tell them to reign it in.

If you were a Christian in the early church and thought tongues were weird and you wanted to join a church that didn't speak in tongues, that wasn't an option.

Today, you can find a church that doesn't believe in tongues, but that wasn't an option for the early church. The early church was birthed out of Pentecost with tongues of fire, and that Pentecostal fire spread to every single church.

Speaking in tongues isn't peripheral to the Spirit-empowered life. It is central to the work and ministry of the Holy Spirit in the life of a believer. It is a practice firmly rooted in Scripture and in the life of the early church.

Since Scripture is the final authority for Christian doctrine and practice, one can embrace speaking in tongues with confidence, knowing that they are walking in step with the Holy Spirit and the authority of God's Word.

PEOPLE ARE NOT THE STANDARD FOR WHAT IS TRUE; GOD'S WORD IS THE STANDARD.

CHAPTER 8

MYTHS & MISCONCEPTIONS

When I first became lead pastor, we had an event called "Encounter"—it was a weekend conference designed to help people experience God's love, find freedom from their past, and walk in His power.

The conference included six sessions, with the final one focused on receiving the Holy Spirit. We invited our church leaders to attend the conference first, so they could help facilitate when we opened it to the rest of the church.

However, a couple of families saw that one session was about speaking in tongues and left before it even began. Afterward, two board members met with me to express their frustration. They told me that if I promised never to talk about speaking in tongues again, they would remain in the church. But if I continued, they would leave.

I was shocked. It wasn't like I was forcing people to speak in tongues. I didn't tell them that they could no longer serve in a leadership capacity if they didn't agree with me on this subject. All I did was teach a message straight from Scripture. After all, speaking in tongues is mentioned throughout the Bible. There's even an entire chapter dedicated to its operation in the local church.

My responsibility as a pastor is to teach the whole counsel of God's Word. It takes the whole Bible to make a whole Christian. But these individuals and their families left our church because I taught a message about speaking in tongues.

Out of all the things I've preached over the years I've never taught anything that causes more controversy or more division than speaking in tongues. Speaking in tongues is one of the most controversial topics in the church.

For many people, speaking in tongues is just a step below snake handling; it's something those crazy Pentecostal Christians do. Others think it's demonic, some people are afraid of it, and others think it's weird; okay, let's be honest, everyone thinks it's weird, including people who speak in tongues.

If you grew up in a church where people spoke in tongues on Sunday mornings and you brought your friend to church, you would pray that someone would not speak in tongues because you didn't want to scare your friend. Sure enough, the lady right behind you would bust out in tongues and scare the mess out of your friend.

Some say it's for today; others believe it passed away. Some think it's from God but only for a select few. And then there are those who say, "I'm not against it—I see it in the Bible—but I've never experienced it, so I don't really understand it."

There are all sorts of different opinions, myths, and misconceptions when it comes to speaking in tongues, so I will share what the Word of God has to say on this subject. Let's take a look at **five common misconceptions about speaking in tongues.**

1. SPEAKING IN TONGUES IS FROM THE DEVIL

Some people believe that speaking in tongues is from the devil. I know a man who once said that if his own mother spoke in tongues, he'd throw her out of his house because it was "from the pit of hell."

But that doesn't make sense—speaking in tongues wasn't the devil's idea. It originated in the mind of God and is listed in Scripture as a gift from God (1 Corinthians 12:10). Not only that, God chose this gift to mark the outpouring of the Holy Spirit on the Day of Pentecost, and it continues to accompany the baptism in the Holy Spirit throughout the Book of Acts.

If tongues were truly from the devil, why doesn't anyone at the bar get drunk and start speaking in tongues? Why isn't there a section at the nightclub for speaking in tongues? Why don't gang members initiate new recruits by having them speak in tongues?

If it's from the devil how come those who are living in rebellion to God are not operating in this gift? Even if you believe tongues are not for today, they can't be from the devil because it was God's idea to begin with.

Now, there are some people who worry about speaking in tongues because they feel like the devil might speak through them, or they might get a demonic spirit. But Jesus addressed that concern:

"If a son asks for bread from any father among you, will he give him a stone? Or if he asks for a fish, will he give him a serpent instead of a fish? Or if he asks for an egg, will he offer him a scorpion? If you then, being evil, know how to give good gifts to your children, how much

more will your heavenly Father give the Holy Spirit to those who ask Him!"
LUKE 11:11-13 NKJV

If you're asking God for the Holy Spirit and the gift of tongues, you don't need to worry about accidentally getting an unholy spirit. God is a good Father—He gives good gifts to His children.

Do counterfeit tongues exist? Yes. The enemy tries to counterfeit everything God creates. But the existence of a counterfeit only proves that the real thing exists. Have you ever seen a counterfeit $6 bill? No—because $6 bills don't exist. You only counterfeit what's authentic and valuable.

Counterfeit tongues are proof that tongues are genuine. However, when you ask God for this gift you don't have to worry about receiving the counterfeit. When you submit yourself to God, He will give you what is holy.

2. SPEAKING IN TONGUES IS SOMETHING ONLY A FEW WEIRD CHRISTIANS DO

Some people think speaking in tongues is something reserved for a few snake-handling Christians living in the mountains of West Virginia—but that's just not true.

There are over 700 million Christians worldwide who pray in tongues. That's one out of every four Christians. The majority of the largest and fastest-growing churches in the world practice speaking in tongues. And it's even more common outside of the United States. If you go on a mission trip to South America or Africa, it doesn't matter what denomination is on the church sign—they speak in tongues.

Still, I've heard people say, "It's just emotionalism. People work themselves into a frenzy and start speaking gibberish."

That argument might hold up if only a handful of people had this experience. But when millions of believers all over the world, across every culture and generation, have experienced something that matches what we see in Scripture—it's hard to write it off as emotional hype or mass hysteria.

> And these signs will follow those who believe:
> In My name they will cast out demons;
> they will speak with new tongues.
> MARK 16:17 NKJV

Jesus said that one of the signs that would follow believers is speaking in tongues, so why do people get so upset about it? Why are people so quick to write this gift off when Jesus said this sign will follow those who believe?

Sometimes people say, "Well, I know someone who speaks in tongues, and they're weird. That's why I don't believe in it."

Some people are just weird. And they'd be weird even if they didn't speak in tongues. Every family has at least one. If you're thinking, *"Not my family,"* then congratulations—*you're* the weird one.

I read a study that said 1 out of every 3 people are weird. So when you are sitting in a row of people and turn to your right and then turn to your left, and the weird person is not one of them, it's you. Some people are just weird. They'd be weird with or without the Holy Spirit. You don't judge the authenticity of tongues based on a few weird people.

What if we judged every doctrine that way? There are some weird Christians who believe in the virgin birth, justification by faith, and the return of Christ, but that doesn't stop me from believing in those truths.

If you are going to judge the baptism in the Holy Spirit and speaking in tongues by some weird people, then you have to judge every doctrine and practice in Christianity that way.

There are a lot of weird Christians who speak in tongues, and there are a lot of dead, lifeless, and religious Christians who don't. God doesn't want dead, lifeless followers, and He doesn't want weird, flakey Christians. Both groups don't represent God's perfect will.

You can't look at someone's life to determine if what they believe is true. People are not the standard for what is true; God's Word is the standard. The Scriptures alone must be the ultimate authority for truth, doctrine, and practice.

3. THE GIFT OF TONGUES HAS PASSED AWAY

I was born at the tail end of Gen X, and the candy we had growing up was...interesting. We had atomic fireballs—jawbreakers that burned your mouth until you spit them out. You had to spit it out after 20 seconds because it was so hot. Pixie sticks—paper straws filled with flavored sugar. It was impossible to eat. You'd try to suck the candy out, but the straw was made of paper, and when it got wet, it would just close. So, we just ended up eating the paper as well.

At some point, straws of sugar weren't enough, so they filled giant plastic tubes with sugar. I wonder how many people almost died from choking on pixie sticks.

We also had wax candies: wax lips and little wax bottles. The bottles came in four different colors, but they all tasted exactly the same. You were supposed to bite off the top and drink the inside, but we just threw the whole thing in our mouths and chewed on it. It was like eating a birthday candle.

Then there were Now & Laters—chewy blocks of candy that you could almost peel the paper off of. What did we do when we couldn't get all the paper off? We ate it. We ate a lot of paper in the '90s.

We had candy jewelry, ring pops, and candy necklaces. The necklaces came on elastic strings you had to stretch to pull over your head, and then you would eat them off your neck. When it was done, you had a rainbow of spit all the way around your neck.

But the worst candy in my generation was candy cigarettes. That's right, they turned cigarettes into candy and bubble gum. There were the candy cigarettes, which were white, hard sticks made of sugar and glue that had no taste whatsoever, and then there were the bubble gum cigarettes, which you could pull out of the pack and blow, and powdered sugar would come out like you were smoking a real cigarette. They were preparing us for addiction when we were kids.

Thankfully, the candy industry has made some improvements over the years. They have eliminated most of the terrible candies I used to eat and replaced them with much better options.

In the same way, some people believe speaking in tongues was available for just one generation—and now it's gone. Like candy cigarettes, they think it's a thing of the past.

When it comes to the gifts of the Spirit, not all Christians agree on how the Holy Spirit works today. The two main theological camps are cessationism and continuationism.

Cessationists believe the gifts of the Spirit were only for the Apostolic Age. They argue that signs and wonders were meant to validate the apostles' message and authority, but once the New Testament was complete, those gifts ceased.

Continuationists, on the other hand, believe the gifts of the Spirit were never meant to be time-limited. They see these gifts as still active today—empowering believers and authenticating the Gospel as we fulfill the church's mission.

Cessationists believe that tongues were only used in the early church, but now that we have the Bible, we no longer need them. So, while at one point in church history, they were a valid gift, they are no longer needed today because we have the New Testament scriptures.

However, the logic behind this argument doesn't make sense. Jesus didn't say, "These signs will follow those who believe until the last apostle dies because then you won't need it anymore." Jesus said one of the signs that would follow believers would be that they would speak in tongues (Mark 16:17).

Tongues marked the birth of the church (Acts 2:4). Throughout the book of Acts, whenever someone was baptized in the Holy Spirit, they spoke in tongues (Acts 2:4, Acts 10:46; Acts 19:6).

The idea that God removed this gift once the Bible was finished doesn't make sense. God didn't say, "I'm going to give you power from on high—but only until you get your hands on a copy of the New Testament." The Bible doesn't replace the need for the Holy Spirit's power.

> **Tongues, miracles, and spiritual gifts have continued from the early church until now.**

If tongues and the other gifts of the Spirit passed away, when did it happen? When was the last day the gifts of the Holy Spirit were in operation? I think it would be a pretty significant day if every manifestation of the Holy Spirit suddenly left the church.

But when you study church history, you won't find that day—because it never happened. Tongues, miracles, and spiritual gifts have continued from the early church until now.

Plus, if these gifts weren't meant for today, why would God devote so much space in 1 Corinthians to teaching about them—especially an entire chapter (1 Corinthians 14) on how to use tongues in the church? Entire chapters of the New Testament are devoted to the gifts so if this only applied to a small group of people for a short period of time it sure is a waste of space in our Bibles.

The primary scriptural argument cessationists use for this theology is found in 1 Corinthians 13—right in between two chapters that talk about the role of tongues in the church:

> "Love never fails. But whether there are prophecies, they will fail; whether there are tongues, they will cease; whether there is knowledge, it will vanish away. For we know in part and we prophesy in part. But when that which is perfect has come, then that which is in part will be done away."
>
> 1 CORINTHIANS 13:8-10 NKJV

People take this verse and see that it says, "Tongues shall cease." That means that speaking in tongues has passed away. They interpret "that which is perfect" to mean the Bible. So once we have the full New Testament, they say, we no longer needed prophecy or tongues.

They teach that God gave the early believers the gifts of healing, miracles, prophesy, and tongues because they didn't have the Bible, but now that we have the Bible, we no longer need these gifts.

But notice in this verse, it says that when tongues cease, knowledge will also cease. Has knowledge ceased? One of the prophecies about the end times is that knowledge will increase (Daniel 12:4). We have access to more knowledge and information at our fingertips than people have had in their entire life.

More knowledge is uploaded to YouTube in one month than all of the knowledge provided by television from its inception until now. Knowledge has not ceased; it's increased. If knowledge hasn't ceased, then prophecy hasn't ceased, and tongues haven't ceased.

"When I was a child, I spoke as a child, I understood as a child, I thought as a child; but when I became a man, I put away childish things. For now we see in a mirror, dimly, but then face to face. Now I know in part, but then I shall know just as I also am known."

1 CORINTHIANS 13:11-12 NKJV

"That which is perfect" refers to the moment we see Jesus face to face. It's not about the completion of the Bible. Paul says that when perfection comes, we will see clearly and know fully—something that hasn't happened yet. When you see Jesus face to face, knowledge will cease because you will know all things, prophecy will cease, and tongues will cease. The only things that will remain are faith, hope, and love.

Yes, tongues will cease—but not until we are with the Lord in eternity. This passage doesn't prove tongues have passed away. It proves the opposite: that we need this gift until we see Jesus face to face.

There's no way someone could read this passage at face value and conclude that tongues aren't for today—unless they went in trying to disprove it.

When people don't see something in their own experience, they often build a theology around what they haven't experienced. That's where cessationism came from—not from Scripture.

Dr. Stephen Crosby, a cessationist, once admitted:

> *"If the Bible was given to an individual with no Christian or biblical exposure whatsoever and the person read it, the individual would not be a Cessationist as a result of the reading. Cessationism is inferential. It must be taught. It is a learned or acquired hermeneutic, not Scripture's self testimony."*

In other words, nobody reading the Bible on their own would come to this conclusion. You have to have someone teach you this false doctrine because it's not in the Bible!

"Therefore, my brothers and sisters, be eager to prophesy, and do not forbid speaking in tongues."
1 CORINTHIANS 14:39 NIV

Paul couldn't be clearer, "Don't tell anyone that they shouldn't speak in tongues." That is pretty straightforward. Do not hinder, stop, or prevent anyone from speaking in tongues. You don't need a theologian to help you understand this verse.

There was a pastor who had been part of a mainline denomination. After he was baptized in the Holy Spirit and spoke in tongues, he was kicked out of both the church and the denomination.

He planted a nondenominational church in the same town. He got a part-time job as a painter to support his family. One day, he was working at a woman's house. This woman was a Christian, and they talked about the Lord. The pastor explained to her that he was raised in the same denomination that she was currently in and how he even used to pastor a church in the denomination but now leads an independent church.

She asked, "Why did you leave?"

He said, "I didn't leave. I got kicked out."

She asked, "Why? Do you speak in tongues?"

"Yes."

She said, "Well, they would've kicked you out of my church too."

The pastor opened his Bible to 1 Corinthians 14:39 and read: *"Do not forbid speaking in tongues."* Then he asked, "How can you forbid something the Bible says not to forbid?"

She shrugged and said, "Well, there are lots of things in the Bible we don't believe."

What do you do with someone who admits they value tradition over Scripture?

How do you reach a person or church who acknowledges that what they believe is contrary to the Word of God but doesn't matter because it's tradition? There are a lot of people who don't let the Bible get in the way of what they believe.

But speaking in tongues didn't pass away with the apostles—because it didn't begin with them. It originated in the heart of God and continues today through the power of the Holy Spirit.

GOD GIVES EVERYONE THE ABILITY TO PRAY IN TONGUES FOR PERSONAL PRAYER.

CHAPTER 9

UNOPENED GIFT

Some believers don't reject the gift of tongues—they just quietly assume it isn't for them. Maybe they've never had the experience, so they figure it must not be their gift. Maybe someone told them tongues is only for a select few, or that it's not that important anyway. Whatever the reason, it's like a beautifully wrapped package that's been sitting unopened. Not because God didn't give it—but because they never realized it had their name on it.

In the last chapter, we confronted some of the biggest theological roadblocks people face when it comes to speaking in tongues. In this chapter, we're going to deal with something even more personal: the doubts that whisper, "This isn't for you."

NOT MY SPIRITUAL GIFT

Many people see from Scripture that speaking in tongues is still for today. They can't deny its validity—not only because millions have experienced it, but because their own close friends have as well. There is no denying its existence and authenticity.

They know the impact that this gift has had in the lives of others, but because they have never spoken in tongues, they just assume that it's not a spiritual gift that God has given them.

> And these signs will follow those who believe: In My name they will cast out demons; they will speak with new tongues; they will take up serpents; and if they drink anything deadly, it will by no means hurt them; they will lay hands on the sick, and they will recover."
>
> MARK 16:17-18 NKJV

Jesus didn't say, "These signs will follow those who have taken a spiritual gift test to determine if they have these gifts." He said, "These signs will follow those who believe." These signs are for all believers.

Do all believers have the authority to cast out devils? Yes. Jesus said, "In my name, they will cast out devils." This isn't just for a special group of believers who are called into deliverance ministry. Every believer can cast out demons.

If a Christian, while out ministering to others, happened to be bitten by a snake or poisoned, would God protect them? Yes. Now, that doesn't mean you play with snakes to prove that they won't hurt you. It just means God promises to protect believers as they are out preaching the Gospel. Is this promise of protection for every believer? Yes.

Can a Christian lay hands on the sick and see them recover? Yes. Every believer can do this. This is not something for a few believers who have been endowed with the gift of healing. It is for every believer.

Can all Christians speak in tongues? When I'm preaching, and I ask this question, most people are afraid to answer. They have no problem answering all the other questions, but with this one, they waver. They aren't sure if everyone can speak in tongues.

Everything else mentioned in this list is for all believers, but tongues often get excluded because of a misunderstanding of what the gift actually is.

> Now you are the body of Christ, and each one of you is a part of it. And God has placed in the church first of all apostles, second prophets, third teachers, then miracles, then gifts of healing, of helping, of guidance, and of different kinds of tongues. Are all apostles? Are all prophets? Are all teachers? Do all work miracles? Do all have gifts of healing? Do all speak in tongues? Do all interpret?
>
> 1 CORINTHIANS 12:27-30 NKJV

Many people read this verse and think, "Well, God gives people different gifts, and this just isn't one that He has given me." But what many people fail to realize is that there are "various kinds of tongues" (1 Corinthians 12:10). There are different kinds of tongues. Scripture points to at least **three distinct types of tongues.**

1. TONGUES AS A SIGN TO UNBELIEVERS.

> Tongues, then, are a sign, not for believers but for unbelievers; prophecy, however, is not for unbelievers but for believers. So if the whole church comes together and everyone speaks in tongues, and inquirers or unbelievers come in, will they not say that you are out of your mind?
>
> 1 CORINTHIANS 14:22-23

This verse sounds like a contradiction. First, it says that tongues are a sign for unbelievers, and then it says that if an unbeliever comes into your church and hears people speaking in tongues, he is going to think everyone is crazy! This sounds like a contradiction, but when you understand that there are different types of tongues, it makes sense.

The first type of tongues we will look at is sign tongues. This is when the Holy Spirit transcends our intellect and gives us the ability to speak in another language that we do not know but that the listener understands. This is what happened on the day of Pentecost.

In Acts 2, they started speaking in tongues, and everyone listening heard them declaring the works of God in their own language. No interpretation was needed because the people heard them speak their native language. The people speaking didn't understand what they were saying, but the people listening did.

There was a man who was quietly speaking in tongues during worship. Unbeknownst to him, there was a professor of linguistics who was standing next to him in worship. The professor approached the man after the service and said, "Where did you learn Sanskrit?" The man said, "I don't know what you mean."

The professor said, "You just spoke the most beautiful Sanskrit. I'm a professor of linguistics, and I heard you speaking in perfect Sanskrit. Where did you learn that?" The man said, "I didn't. I was speaking in tongues."

The professor said, "No, that is impossible. Where did you learn it?" The man explained that it was a gift of the Spirit, and then he asked the professor what he had been saying in tongues. The professor said, "You were saying, God is truth, God is light, this is the way to God."

The professor was a Hare Krishna, and that night, he gave his life to Christ because he heard someone preaching the Gospel to him in a language he knew, but it was unknown to the person speaking. This is why it says tongues are a sign for unbelievers.

2. TONGUES FOR INTERPRETATION

How is it then, brethren? Whenever you come together, each of you has a psalm, has a teaching, has a tongue, has a revelation, has an interpretation. Let all things be done for edification. If anyone speaks in a tongue, let there be two or at the most three, each in turn, and let one interpret.

1 CORINTHIANS 14:26-27 NKJV

We will call this the **public gift**. This is not tongues as a sign to an unbeliever but tongues for interpretation. This is when there is a corporate church gathering, and someone gets up and speaks in an unknown language, and since no one knows what they are saying, they need to be interpreted.

Interpretation of tongues is another gift in which the Spirit enables you to understand a message in tongues even without any knowledge of the language being spoken. They then declare the interpretation to the church so that the church may be edified.

When someone speaks in tongues as a sign to unbelievers, no interpretation is needed because it's not a message for the corporate church body; it's a message to one person who understands the language being spoken.

But here, it says that if someone speaks in tongues in a corporate church setting, there needs to be an interpretation so that it will edify the people present. The purpose of this gift is not to witness to unbelievers. It is to encourage and edify the church.

3. TONGUES FOR PERSONAL PRAYER

For he who speaks in a tongue does not speak to men but to God, for no one understands him; however, in the spirit he speaks mysteries.

1 CORINTHIANS 14:2 NKJV

We will call this the **private gift.** The type of speaking in tongues mentioned in this verse is different from the ones we previously mentioned because it is not directed toward people but to God. Sign tongues are speaking to an unbeliever. The gift of tongues is speaking to the church, but this type speaks not to people but to God.

The first two types of tongues are for public use, but here, Paul is talking about tongues for private prayer. The other two gifts are for speaking to people, but in this kind, you are praying to God in a language you don't understand.

You don't need to have an interpretation during your private prayer time because you're speaking to God, and He understands what you're saying. In the spirit, you're speaking mysteries, which means you don't have a clue what you're saying.

It wouldn't be a mystery if you were to interpret your tongue. So, you do not need to interpret when you speak in tongues for private prayer or in a semi-private setting, like during worship or in a corporate prayer meeting.

In such a setting, an interpretation is not needed since the tongue is not intended to be a public message but rather for your own personal edification.

He who speaks in a tongue edifies himself, but he who

prophesies edifies the church.
1 CORINTHIANS 14:4 NKJV

When you speak in tongues, you edify yourself, but the other two types edify others.

Tongues for interpretation benefits the church. Tongues for a sign benefits unbelievers. Tongues for personal prayer benefits you.

This is why God gives everyone the ability to pray in tongues for personal prayer. He wants everyone to have the ability to strengthen and build themselves up.

As you can see, there are different types of tongues that have different purposes.

DO ALL SPEAK IN TONGUES?

Now you are the body of Christ, and each one of you is a part of it. And God has placed in the church first of all apostles, second prophets, third teachers, then miracles, then gifts of healing, of helping, of guidance, and of different kinds of tongues. Are all apostles? Are all prophets? Are all teachers? Do all work miracles? Do all have gifts of healing? Do all speak in tongues? Do all interpret?
1 CORINTHIANS 12:27-30 NKJV

When Paul said, "Do all speak in tongues," he wasn't talking about tongues for personal prayer; he was referring to tongues for interpretation. He was referring to the public gift of tongues, not tongues for private prayer. Not everyone has the public gift, but everyone can speak in tongues for their own private prayer life.

Are all prophets? No, but could any Christian be used in the gift of prophecy? Yes (1 Corinthians 14:31). Do all have the gift of healing? No, but can any believer lay hands on the sick and see them recover? Yes (Mark 16:17-18).

Are all appointed as teachers in the body of Christ? No, but you can teach someone something you've learned from God's Word (1 Corinthians 14:26). Are all believers called to hold the office of an evangelist? No (Ephesians 4:11), but that doesn't mean you can't lead someone to Christ or share the Gospel.

In the same way, not everyone will have the gift of tongues for interpretation. However, everyone can pray in tongues during their own personal prayer time when they are baptized in the Holy Spirit.

God gives everyone the ability to pray in tongues for personal prayer.

One gift is for public use, and the other is for private use. The difference between those who have a public gift and those who have a private gift is the difference between those who sing publicly and those who sing privately.

I used to love watching *American Idol*, not because I loved seeing people fulfill their dreams, but because I loved seeing people bomb on national television. My favorite part of the show was the first round of auditions.

People who thought they could sing would confidently stand in front of the judges and start singing, and they were absolutely terrible. The judges would rip these people apart. I loved it.

So, while these people could sing privately, their gift was never meant to be shared publicly. Everyone can sing, but not everyone should record or do it publicly.

In the same way, everyone can pray in tongues privately, but not everyone has the gift to do it publicly. You don't need the public gift of tongues to pray in private any more than you need the public gift to sing in order to sing praises to God.

I don't have the gift of tongues. I've never given a message in tongues in a public meeting, but I pray in tongues every single day in my own personal prayer life. While not everyone will have the public gift, everyone can pray in tongues when they are baptized in the Holy Spirit.

That is why Acts 2, 10, and 19 say that they all spoke in tongues when they were baptized in the Spirit. Whenever it mentions someone speaking in tongues as a result of the baptism in the Holy Spirit, it says, "They all spoke in tongues." It doesn't say only a few spoke—it says they all did. Praying in tongues is a function of the baptism in the Holy Spirit and therefore available to all.

The Apostle Paul said, "I wish you all spoke in tongues" (1 Corinthians 14:5). If not everyone can, why would Paul say that? Why would he desire something that's outside the will of God—and why would God allow that desire to be included in His holy, inerrant Word?

In Mark 16:17, Jesus said one of the signs that will follow believers is that they will speak in tongues. Just as all believers can cast out demons and lay hands on the sick, every believer can speak in tongues.

When something is clearly stated in the Word but not reflected in your life, you have two choices: You can lower God's

Word to match your experience, or you can humble yourself and ask God to raise your experience to match His Word.

You can say, "Well, I don't speak in tongues, so it must not be for everyone." Or you can pray, "Lord, You said this sign will follow those who believe—and I believe. What You promised is for me, and I won't stop seeking until it becomes my reality."

You can either lower God's Word to match your current experience or humble yourself and ask God to raise your experience to match His Word.

THE LEAST OF THE GIFTS

Most Christians don't deny the existence of tongues today. They realize it is a legitimate spiritual gift, but they don't seek this gift because they were told that it is the least of all the gifts of the Spirit. They were taught to downplay its importance.

> "I wish you all spoke with tongues, but even more that you prophesied; for he who prophesies is greater than he who speaks with tongues, unless indeed he interprets, that the church may receive edification."
> 1 CORINTHIANS 14:5 NKJV

People take this verse to mean that Paul is saying, "It's okay if you speak in tongues, but it's better for you to prophesy because prophecy is better than tongues." Many people have falsely concluded that tongues are the least of the gifts.

I'll show you in a minute that's not what Paul was communicating, but even if it were the least, it would still be greater than anything we could do in our own strength. The least of God's gifts is better than the best of ours.

However, Paul wasn't trying to diminish tongues—he was teaching the Corinthians how to use it properly in a corporate setting.

Remember, Paul was writing to correct the excessive use of tongues in their corporate gatherings. I believe that the church in Corinth saw what happened on Pentecost. All the believers spoke in tongues, and the people heard them declaring the works of God in their own language. And they were trying to reproduce sign tongues in their services so everyone was speaking in tongues, which was chaotic.

This whole chapter is about exercising spiritual gifts in the context of a local church. It does not diminish the gift of tongues; he states that everything done in a corporate church service should edify and encourage everyone, not just the individual speaking in tongues.

In a corporate setting, it's better to speak in a language people understand. If no one understands what's being said, no one is edified—except the person speaking.

The Apostle Paul wasn't saying that prophecy is more spiritual than tongues. He was saying that, in public ministry, clarity matters. It's better to speak in a way people can understand than in tongues that require interpretation.

This doesn't apply to personal prayer. It's about using this gift in a public setting. And in that setting, it's better to speak in words people can understand than in tongues.

This is why, on Sunday morning, you don't see people getting up and speaking in tongues on a microphone even though all of our staff speak in tongues. In this setting, it's better to use words people can understand, but that doesn't mean tongues are not a powerful gift. It has tremendous value for personal prayer life.

There was a small group leader who left her apartment to head to a meeting when she suddenly felt a strong burden to pray. She didn't know what for, so she began praying in tongues.

After a while, the burden lifted, and she went to her group as planned. When she returned home after the meeting, her house had been broken into. Looking for things of value in her home, the thief threw clothes and other things all over the floor.

Yet, something strange happened. Her jewelry and cash, which were not hidden, were untouched. Somehow, the thief had been blinded to the obvious things of value in her apartment and left without taking anything.

Even though she didn't know what she was praying for, when she prayed in tongues, God used those prayers to keep the person who broke into her house from stealing anything.

This gift not only has tremendous value when used correctly in a church service, but it is also a powerful gift in your personal prayer life.

OUT OF ALL THE GIFTS OF HEAVEN, THERE IS NOTHING MORE VALUABLE, BENEFICIAL, AND IMPORTANT FOR THE HOLY SPIRIT TO GIVE TO US THAN OUR OWN PRAYER LANGUAGE.

CHAPTER 10

SUPERNATURAL COMMUNICATION

At this point we've already established that the gift of tongues is still in operation today. It's not a gift for a select few. It's given to every single person when they are baptized in the Holy Spirit.

But many people still wonder why anyone would need this gift? Or why would God choose such a strange gift? Think about it, God chose this gift to mark the beginning of the church. He chose this gift to be the initial sign that someone received the Holy Spirit.

Why did God do this? This gift is not only weird, but it's also the most controversial and divisive gift of the spirit. From the first moment people started speaking in tongues, there was confusion and controversy.

"So they were all amazed and perplexed, saying to one another, "Whatever could this mean?" Others mocking said, "They are full of new wine."
ACTS 2:12-13 NKJV

When the Holy Spirit was poured out and they started speaking in tongues, some people were amazed, others perplexed, a little confused thinking "What is going on?" while others said, "They are drunk." There's been division over tongues from the start.

Why would God birth the church with such a controversial gift and then institute this gift in the life of every believer who is filled with the Spirit? God could have given the gift of healing, prophecy, or the working of miracles, but He didn't. God chose the gift of tongues. Why? Because the gift of tongues is the greatest gift the Holy Spirit could give.

If you wanted to give someone you really love a gift and money wasn't an issue, you would give them the best possible gift. You won't shop at the dollar store; you will give them the greatest gift you could afford. The same is true with the Holy Spirit which is why He gives us the gift of tongues.

God the Father, Son, and Holy Spirit each gave us the best possible gift they could give. God the Father's best gift was His Son. "For God so loved the world that He gave His only begotten son" (John 3:16).

Jesus the Son gave us His best gift, the Holy Spirit. "It is to your advantage that I go away; for if I do not go away, the Helper will not come to you; but if I depart, I will send Him to you" (John 16:7).

The Holy Spirit gave us the best gift He could give: the gift of tongues. That's why I believe tongues are a provision of the baptism in the Holy Spirit—it's the best gift the Spirit could give.

Out of all the gifts of heaven, there is nothing more valuable, beneficial, and important for the Holy Spirit to give to us than our own prayer language.

God could have chosen any other gift, but He chose tongues. Why? In order to communicate, you need language. Our ability to communicate is dependent on the language we possess.

Years ago, I went on a mission trip to China. I only knew a couple phrases, "nǐ hǎo" which is *hello* and "xiè xiè" which means *thank you.* Those were the only words I knew, which meant my ability to communicate was extremely limited.

However, when I went to Nicaragua, they spoke Spanish. I knew a little more Spanish. I took two years of Spanish in high school so I could hold a basic conversation with someone. "¿Dónde está el baño?"

In order to connect, we need to speak a common language. The depth of relationship one can experiences is dependent upon having a shared language. This is what speaking in tongues is all about.

Imagine trying to communicate your deepest thoughts, feelings, and dreams but lacking the words to truly communicate what's on your heart. This is why God gave us the gift of tongues: to ensure we're never at a loss for words when pouring out our hearts to Him.

When you are baptized in the Holy Spirit, you are given a new language to communicate with God. This spiritual language bridges the gap between human limitation and divine communication. This gift is not merely about speaking in another language but about receiving a new way to communicate with God that transcends earthly barriers. It allows you to communicate with God without constraint, enabling you to communicate beyond what you can express or comprehend. It provides a continuous and inexhaustible means of communicating with God.

Tongues may be controversial to some, but it's crystal clear in Scripture—God gave this gift on purpose, and He gave it for you.

THE BEST COMMUNICATION

When you get married, one of the first things you have to learn is how your spouse communicates. And that takes time—because men and women don't speak the same language.

> **God gave us the gift of tongues to ensure we're never at a loss for words when pouring out our hearts to Him.**

It took me a couple of years into our marriage before I realized something: my wife will never *tell* me to do anything around the house. If she wants me to do something, she'll ask a question.

I then have to reverse engineer the question to figure out what she's actually trying to say. Let's say I leave a pair of underwear on the floor. She doesn't say, "Pick those up." Three simple words—I would know exactly what to do.

But no. That would be too easy. That would be clear, direct, and—dare I say it—logical. We'd be communicating at the highest human level: actual language. The way God intended.

Instead, she looks at me and says, "Are those yours?"

I *hope* they are. If not, I have a few questions of my own.

Women communicate in code. So, guys, let me help you decipher it:

If she says, "Do whatever you want"—don't do whatever you want. She does not mean that. Do the opposite of what you want to do.

If you ask, "Are you okay?" and she says, "I'm fine"—she is not fine. She is angry with you.

If you ask, "What's wrong?" and she says, "Nothing"—there is definitely something. "Nothing" always means "something."

How do you know if a woman is mad at you? Easy. If she's silent, if she's yelling, if she's acting different, or if she's acting the same—she's mad at you.

If you ask, "Can I go play golf with my friends for the third weekend in a row?" and she says, "Go ahead"—that's not permission. That's a dare. Don't fall for it.

And if you do something and she says, "Wow!"—that is not a compliment. She is not impressed. She is shocked that you could actually be that stupid.

Communication is hard. That's why God gave us a supernatural language to talk to Him—speaking in tongues.

Dr. Andrew Newberg, a neuroscientist known for studying the brain and religious experiences, conducted a fascinating study on people who speak in tongues. Using brain imaging, he observed what was happening in the brain while individuals were actively praying in tongues.

He found there was decreased activity in the frontal lobe—the area of the brain responsible for decision-making, self-control, self-awareness, and speech.

Dr. Newberg compared brain scans of Christians praying in tongues with those of monks meditating and Catholic nuns praying. The results were noticeably different. For the monks and nuns, the frontal lobe lit up with activity. But for those speaking in tongues, that same region of the brain went quiet.

In other words, the areas of the brain that control language and speech weren't active during tongues. This supports the idea that speaking in tongues is different from typical speech.

Even if you were just making up words, the portion of your brain that controls speech would be activated, but speaking in tongues does not use the same portion of your brain that you use in normal speech. It is a supernatural language that doesn't come from your natural mind; it comes from your spirit.[1]

There was a boy who had a speech impediment and could not articulate the letter "R." Any word that had the letter "R" in it, he could not pronounce correctly. No matter how hard he tried, he could not say that letter.

Then, he got baptized in the Holy Spirit and spoke in tongues. When speaking in tongues he could pronounce every word with an "R" perfectly. When he tried to speak in English again, he still could not pronounce "R."

Speaking in tongues does not come from the part of your brain that controls speech.

He would try speaking in tongues and then quickly changing over to English and pronounce "R," but it didn't work. He could only pronounce words with the letter "R" while speaking in tongues.

Speaking in tongues does not come from the part of your brain that controls speech. That is exactly what the Bible teaches.

For if I pray in a tongue, my spirit prays,
but my mind is unfruitful.
1 CORINTHIANS 14:14 NKJV

When we pray in tongues, our prayers originate from the spirit, not the natural mind. This is a supernatural language God has given us to communicate with Him.

LANGUAGE OF THE SPIRIT

In Genesis chapter 11, the whole world had one common language, and they decided to build a tower to reach heaven and make a name for themselves.

> The Lord said, "If as one people speaking the same language they have begun to do this, then nothing they plan to do will be impossible for them. Come, let us go down and confuse their language so they will not understand each other."
>
> GENESIS 11:6-7 NIV

Because these people all spoke the same language, God said, "Nothing will be impossible for them." So, God took away the one language they possessed and gave them all different languages. This is why different parts of the world speak different languages.

> For then I will restore to the peoples a pure language, that they all may call on the name of the Lord, to serve Him with one accord.
>
> ZEPHANIAH 3:9 NKJV

Zephaniah prophesies that there will be a day when God will restore a pure language. I believe this pure language is the language of heaven that they spoke before the tower of Babel.

Notice He didn't say God would "give a pure language" or "create a pure language." He said, "restore." To restore means to bring back or reinstate.[2] So God is saying that a day is coming when He will restore a pure language to His people so that they may serve God with one accord.

When the Day of Pentecost had fully come, they were all with one accord in one place. And suddenly there came a sound from heaven, as of a rushing mighty wind, and it filled the whole house where they were sitting. Then there appeared to them divided tongues, as of fire, and one sat upon each of them. And they were all filled with the Holy Spirit and began to speak with other tongues, as the Spirit gave them utterance. And there were dwelling in Jerusalem Jews, devout men, from every nation under heaven and when this sound occurred, the multitude came together, and were confused, because everyone heard them speak in his own language.

ACTS 2:1-5 NKJV

On the day of Pentecost, every nation under heaven was present. All the nations that were scattered in Genesis 11 had been gathered back together in one city. In Acts 2, we see the reversal of the tower of Babel.

At the Tower of Babel, God gave different languages to divide the nations. At Pentecost, God gave back one common language to unite every nation. God restored one language, but this time, it was a language of the spirit—a pure language, undefiled by the mind, will, and emotions.

At the Tower of Babel, one language was taken away; at Pentecost, one language was restored. Remember when they had one common language? God said, "Nothing is impossible for these people." God gave us one language again to unite us so that nothing would be impossible.

This is why the enemy fights against tongues. He does not want the people of God praying in a unified language. Speaking in tongues is one of the most divisive issues in the church when it was meant to unify us by giving us one common language. The enemy uses the very thing that was meant to unify to bring division. Because when people are unified in both language and purpose, nothing is impossible for them.

SPEAKING IN TONGUES BYPASSES OUR MIND ALLOWING US TO PRAY THE PERFECT WILL OF GOD.

CHAPTER 11

THE BENEFITS

John G. Lake was a missionary whose life was marked by extraordinary signs and wonders. He operated in a remarkable level of spiritual authority and power.

In his initial 18 months as a missionary in South Africa, Lake planted over 100 churches. At the end of his five years of ministry in that nation, he left behind 1250 preachers, 625 churches, over 100,000 new converts, and countless testimonies of miraculous healings.

Then, he moved back to the United States to Spokane, Washington, and set up a ministry school of healing. In its initial 5 years of existence, the school documented and recorded over 100,000 healings. The government actually investigated what had become known as the "Healing Rooms" and gave this report: "Rev. Lake, through divine healing, has made Spokane the healthiest city in the world, according to United States statistics."

What was the secret of John G. Lake's spiritual power? To what did he attribute the success of his ministry? Praying in tongues. John G. Lake said, "Tongues has been the making of my ministry."

The reason why there is so much controversy and division over this gift is because the enemy knows the power that is available through speaking in tongues, and he does not want believers to access all the wonderful benefits that come from praying in tongues.

SUPERNATURAL PRAYER

Have you ever been in prayer and you didn't know what to pray for? Or maybe you were facing a situation, and you knew what to pray for, but you didn't know how to pray about it? Knowing what and how to pray can be a struggle.

How would you like to pray God's perfect will of God every time you pray? That's exactly what happens when you pray in tongues. It's a supernatural act that bypasses your mind, allowing you to pray the perfect will of God.

For if I pray in a tongue, my spirit prays, but my understanding is unfruitful.

1 CORINTHIANS 14:14 NKJV

People say, "Speaking in tongues is weird. I don't understand what I'm saying." That's the point. The very thing that makes tongues weird is the same thing that makes it powerful. Most of our problems are right between our ears. Our thinking and understanding are the problem. So, God bypasses our mind, allowing us to pray the perfect will of God.

When we pray in our native language, we pray according to our understanding. The problem is that our understanding is limited, our perspective is incomplete, and our judgments are often clouded by our experiences and biases. This means that when we pray, we don't always pray in line with God's perfect will.

There are times when I pray, and I think I know what the problem is, but I'm way off. I think my problem is my wife, but it's really me. I think my problem is my kids, but it's really my attitude. I think my problem is that person, but it's really my pride and ego.

Because I think those things are the problem, I pray and ask God to change them. "God, change my wife, change my kids, change that person because they are getting on my nerves." That's what happens often when we pray according to our understanding. We miss the mark.

You ask and do not receive because you ask amiss.
JAMES 4:3 NKJV

When we pray according to our understanding, we often miss the mark, and we miss out on receiving answers to our prayers.

However, when we pray in tongues, our spirit prays. We don't pray from our understanding, intellect, emotions, or will. We pray from our spirit. Speaking in tongues bypasses our mind allowing us to pray the perfect will of God.

When you pray in the spirit, you think you are praying to change your spouse but are really praying, "God, change me." You think you are praying for God to change the rebellious teenager, but you are really praying, "God help me love them the way you love them." You think you are praying, "God, change that person," but you are really praying, "God, change my heart towards that person."

When you pray in tongues, you pray the perfect will of God every single time. When you pray with your understanding, you pray according to your will. But when you pray in tongues, you pray according to God's will.

A father was trying to teach his daughter how to pray. Before they went to bed, they prayed together. The first night, he prayed, and she repeated after him. The second night, she started to pray her own prayers, and she prayed for her mom, dad, friends, and grandparents.

The third night, he lets her pray on her own, and he listens from outside the door and hears, "ABCDEFG…" He hears her singing the alphabet song, so he laughs and goes on his way. The next night, he listened to her prayer again, and he heard, "ABCDEFG..." He walked into the room and said, "Sweetie, what are you doing." She said, "Praying." He said, "No, you're not praying. You're just singing the alphabet," She said, "Daddy, I am praying. I'm giving God the letters so He can arrange them however He wants."

That is essentially what you're doing when you pray in tongues. You are surrendering your tongue to God and allowing Him to arrange the words and syllables as He sees fit. Leave it to God to hide such immense power in such a childlike act.

You are praying for more money to come in for your business, but God knows you need more people, and if you get the right people, the money will come, so when you pray in the spirit, you pray for God to send the right people.

You keep praying for the promotion at work, but God doesn't want you to climb the ladder in that company. He wants you to start your own business, so while you think you're praying about your current job, you are actually praying for the business you'll start.

You are praying for your prodigal child to come back to the Lord. You are praying that your words will get through to them, but God knows that they've tuned you out. It's going to take someone else speaking into their life to bring them back to the Lord. When you pray in tongues, you are asking God to send godly people across their path.

Every other prayer you pray is filtered through your perception, experiences, judgments, opinions, and limited understanding, but when you pray in tongues, you align your prayers with God's will every single time.

Look at how Paul describes the partnership of the Spirit in our prayer life in Romans:

> Likewise the Spirit also helps in our weaknesses. For we do not know what we should pray for as we ought, but the Spirit Himself makes intercession for us with groanings which cannot be uttered. Now He who searches our hearts knows what the mind of the Spirit is, because He makes intercession for the saints according to the will of God.
>
> ROMANS 8:26-27 NKJV

Dr. Bruce Metzger was a professor at Princeton Theological Seminary. He was considered to be one of the greatest Greek scholars and textual critics. He was a cessationist who did not believe speaking in tongues was for today. However, when asked what Paul was referring to in this passage from Romans 8. Metzger surprisingly responded, "Praying in tongues."

The Holy Spirit helps when we do not know what to pray for. He intercedes through us as we pray in tongues. One of our biggest weaknesses is our lack of knowledge. We don't know what we don't know. How can you pray about something you have no knowledge of? How can you pray about the future when you have no knowledge of the future? Even when we know what to pray about, we don't know how to pray as we should.

Thankfully, the Holy Spirit helps us pray when we don't know what to pray for. When you pray in tongues, the Holy Spirit helps you by praying the perfect will of God through you.

There are times when we need to pray for something, but we don't know we need to pray for it. We don't just pray amiss; we don't pray at all because we don't know that we need to pray for it. However, when you pray in tongues, you can intercede for things you have no knowledge of.

Lester Summerall was a missionary in Tibet. He would travel through the hills and mountains, going from village to village, preaching the Gospel. One time, while traveling, he got severely sick. He was so sick that he passed out and fell off his donkey.

He was in the middle of nowhere, hours away from any hospital. Nobody knew where he was or that he was in trouble. He lay unconscious on the ground for a couple of hours and then woke up completely healed. Moreover, his donkey was still standing there. He got on the donkey and went to the next village, preaching the Gospel.

When you pray in tongues, you can intercede for things you have no knowledge of.

A couple of months later, he was back in the United States, preaching at a church, testifying of God's healing power. After the service, a woman approached him and asked him exactly when that happened.

He told her the date and time it happened, and she opened up her journal and showed him the date and time when God woke her up in the middle of the night to pray for him, and it was the exact same day and time that he fell off the donkey.

She didn't know what to pray because she had no idea what was going on, so she prayed in tongues. As she prayed in the spirit, she prayed the perfect will of God for Lester Summerall.

When you pray in tongues, you can pray for things you have no knowledge of because the Holy Spirit makes intercession through us according to the will of God. When you're faced with a problem that you don't understand, you can pray in the language you don't understand and allow the Holy Spirit to pray through you.

Sometimes, you'll sense a burden to pray, but you don't know what you're supposed to pray for. Or you'll get a feeling that you're supposed to pray for someone, but you don't know what's going on, but you can pray in the spirit and intercede for them according to the will of God.

If you feel a burden to pray but don't know what to pray, just pray in the spirit until you feel a release to stop or until you feel peace. Sometimes, it takes 10 minutes. Other times, it may take one hour. However long it takes, pray until you sense a breakthrough.

PROACTIVE PRAYERS

Far too often, we pray reactive prayers. We pray for healing after the car accident. We pray for finances after the bill shows up. We pray for the prodigal after they've walked away from the Lord.

When you pray in tongues, you pray proactive prayers. Tongues lets you get ahead of the problem. You can prevent disaster, hardship, and calamity before it strikes.

One night, Allen had a dream. In the dream, he heard the doorbell ring and went to open the door. There was a state trooper at the door who said, "Do you have a daughter named Jill?" He said, "Yes." The state trooper said, "Was she with a man named Rodrick?" He said, "Yes." The state trooper said, "I'm sorry to inform you, but they have both been killed in a car accident."

After this dream, he woke up at 1:30 a.m. He immediately started praying in tongues until he felt a sense of peace, and then he went back to bed. Then, the next day, he talked to his daughter and said, "How was your trip?"

She said, "You won't believe it. Rodrick was driving, and I was asleep in the car. When I woke up, I noticed that Rodrick had fallen asleep while driving! I grabbed the steering wheel and woke him up. Then we pulled over, and I drove the rest of the way." Allen said, "What time did that happen?" She said, "Around 1:30 in the morning." That was the exact same time he woke up and began to pray in tongues.

Praying in tongues allows you to shift from praying reactively to praying proactively. By praying in the spirit, you can prevent accidents, calamities, and problems. You can stop problems before they even start.

People get hung up on the fact that they don't understand what they're praying, but you don't have to understand something in order to benefit from it. I don't understand how a brown cow can eat green grass and make white milk, but that doesn't stop me from drinking milk.

You can benefit from something even if you don't understand it. Although you don't know what you're praying for, you can experience the benefits of praying the perfect will of God every time you pray in tongues.

When you pray in your native language, you can only pray according to your understanding and knowledge of the situation, but when you pray in the spirit, you are able to transcend your understanding and proactively pray the perfect will of God. You are able to pray according to God's wisdom and knowledge.

When you pray in tongues, you pray perfect prayers because it bypasses your mind as you pray according to the mind of God.

SUPERNATURAL DIRECTION

> When we put bits into the mouths of horses to make them obey us, we can turn the whole animal. Or take ships as an example. Although they are so large and are driven by strong winds, they are steered by a very small rudder wherever the pilot wants to go. Likewise, the tongue is a small part of the body, but it makes great boasts.
>
> JAMES 3:3-5 NKJV

The first time I went horseback riding I was about 7 and I went with my family to Mt. Charleston. We found a place that took you on a little trail through the mountains. They gave me this horse called, "Booger" and they said, "This horse is real calm. He won't give you any problems; he will just follow the horse in front of him."

We get on the trail and we are slowly walking through the mountains. Everything is calm and peaceful when suddenly Booger loses his mind and starts running off the trail through the forest. I'm screaming at the top of my lungs worried this demon-possessed horse is going to run off a cliff. I have no idea how to stop him. All I can do is yell, 'Stop!'—but nothing is working! He is still running and then suddenly he stops at these yellow flowers and starts eating them. This horse almost killed me over some flowers.

I didn't ride a horse for another 15 years because I was so traumatized. Now, the second time I went horseback riding I was a lot older, but these horses weren't nice tame trail horses. They were wild horses that were tamed by a man who drank way too much alcohol because all his horses were named after beer. He was riding "Bud Light." My brother was riding "Corona," and I'm riding "Keystone." CJ the owner said, "If this horse starts giving you problems then you take this rein and you pull on it and make him walk in a circle to show him who's boss."

I'm thinking, "I'm not the boss. This 1,200lb horse is the boss." We start riding and suddenly Keystone sped up. I didn't want to go that fast so I pulled on the reins and make him go in a circle and he slowed down. And every time he would try to speed up or do something I didn't want him to do, I would show him who was boss and make him walk around in a circle.

With that tiny piece of metal in the horse's mouth I could control the horse's direction. Just like a bit steers a horse, your tongue steers your life. Your tongue will control the direction of your life. Your tongue will set the course for your life. Like a rudder on your ship, your tongue will determine the direction of your life. Whatever direction your tongue is pointing your life will follow. Your life is moving in the direction of your words, but there is one major problem.

The tongue also is a fire, a world of evil among the parts of the body. It corrupts the whole body, sets the whole course of one's life on fire, and is itself set on fire by hell. All kinds of animals, birds, reptiles and sea creatures are being tamed and have been tamed by mankind, but no

human being can tame the tongue.
JAMES 3:6-7 NIV

Your tongue will determine the direction of your life, but the problem is that it's a world of evil. How much trouble has your tongue gotten you into? My elbow never caused me any problems. My collarbone has never gotten me into trouble. But my tongue? That thing's gotten me into all kinds of trouble.

The tongue is a world of evil, set on fire by hell, and it cannot be tamed. That's a huge problem. The very thing that steers the course of your life is ignited by hell and beyond human control. In other words, it will take divine intervention to bring it under submission.

When the Holy Spirit came on the day of Pentecost tongues of fire rested on each of them and All of them were filled with the Holy Spirit and began to speak in other tongues as the Spirit enabled them.
ACTS 2:4 NKJV

In James we're told the tongue is set on fire by hell but in Acts 2, we see it set on fire by heaven. Notice the very first thing the Holy Spirit did when he came. He changed their tongue because your tongue sets the course and direction of your life. If the Holy Spirit can get a hold of your tongue, He can set the course and direction of your life.

When you speak in tongues, the Holy Spirit begins to direct the course of your life, leading you into God's perfect will.

Now, do you understand why there is so much controversy around speaking in tongues? The enemy knows the power of your words. He understands that if your tongue is tamed by the Holy Spirit and you speak words inspired by the Spirit of God, you can set the course of your life in a new direction and walk in the destiny and purpose God has for you.

The enemy knows the power of this gift which is why he fights so adamantly against it because he knows that when your tongue is submitted to the Holy Spirit it will completely change the course of your life.

How many apps do you have on your phone that you've never even opened? You downloaded them because someone said, "This will change your life!" It'll manage your money, plan your meals, coach your workouts, teach you Spanish, and even generate a grocery list based on your DNA and seasonal produce. There's even an AI assistant now that'll schedule your meetings, optimize your sleep, and remind you to drink water. But you never opened it. You just let it sit there, quietly judging you from your home screen.

That's what a lot of believers do with the gift of tongues.

When you were baptized in the Holy Spirit, this spiritual app got downloaded into your life. It's loaded with supernatural power. It gives you access to divine wisdom, heavenly strategy, and God's perfect will—stuff you don't have on your own. But it doesn't run in the background. You have to open it. You have to use it.

Don't let it just sit there. Activate it—and watch what happens when heaven's wisdom starts working through your words.

THE HOLY SPIRIT WILL NOT FORCE HIMSELF ON YOU. HE'S WAITING FOR YOUR INVITATION.

CHAPTER 12

RECEIVING THE HOLY SPIRIT

A Christian lady went downstairs one evening and was surprised to see a burglar in her kitchen. He was all loaded down with the things he was going to steal. She had no weapon and was all alone. The only thing that she could think of doing was to quote Scripture. So, she held up her hand and said, "Acts 2:38!"

The burglar froze in fear and didn't move. She grabbed the phone and called the police. When the police arrived, the burglar was still frozen in the same place. The police were surprised this woman could keep the thief from moving without a weapon.

One of the officers asked, "How did you do this?" The woman replied, "I quoted Scripture!" The officer turned to the burglar and asked, "What was it about the scripture that had such an effect on you?" The burglar replied, "Scripture! What Scripture?" The police officer said, "Acts 2:38." The burglar said, "I thought she said she had an axe and two 38s!"

Now, while that burglar may have misunderstood Acts 2:38 for an axe and two .38s, there's real power in what that verse actually says.

Then Peter said to them, "Repent, and let every one of you be baptized in the name of Jesus Christ for the remission of sins; and you shall receive the gift of the Holy Spirit.
ACTS 2:38 NKJV

God wants every person to experience these three things: salvation, water baptism, and the Holy Spirit. Having seen that the baptism in the Holy Spirit follows salvation, let's talk about how a person receives the Holy Spirit.

It's important to see that Peter called it "the gift of the Holy Spirit." If something is a gift, that means it's freely given. It cannot be earned by good behavior, and you can't be disqualified from receiving it for your bad behavior.

Many people think they have to achieve some standard of holiness before they can receive the Spirit. I've heard pastors say, "The Holy Spirit won't fill a dirty vessel, so if you want to receive the Spirit, you have to get your life cleaned up."

The Holy Spirit isn't a reward for holy living. He is the means by which we become holy.

However, you don't clean up your life to receive the Spirit; receiving the Spirit is how you clean up your life. If you could get rid of all the sin in your life without the Spirit's help, then you wouldn't need Him. The Holy Spirit is not the prize for cleaning up our lives; He is our only chance at cleaning up our lives.

The Holy Spirit isn't a reward for holy living. He is the means by which we become holy. This gift empowers us to be like Jesus.

But like any gift, He must be received. So the question is how do we receive the gift of the Holy Spirit?

REQUEST

Some churches teach that if you want to receive the Holy Spirit, you need to **tarry**, which means *to wait*. They even hold "tarry services" where believers gather for extended times of prayer, waiting to be baptized in the Holy Spirit. I've heard pastors tell stories about tarrying at the altar for hours—or even months—before they were finally filled with the Spirit.

The concept of tarrying comes from Luke 24:49 (KJV), where Jesus tells His disciples, "Tarry ye in the city of Jerusalem, until ye be endued with power from on high." But the only reason they had to wait was because the Holy Spirit hadn't been poured out yet. The disciples waited ten days in the upper room because the gift hadn't been given.

But after the Day of Pentecost, that changed. The Holy Spirit was poured out so we don't have to wait anymore—we just have to ask.

> If you then, being evil, know how to give good gifts to your children, how much more will your heavenly Father give the Holy Spirit to those who ask Him!
>
> LUKE 11:13 NKJV

One time, I was on a flight headed to Atlanta. As we approached the airport, there wasn't a clear runway for us to land, so they put us in a holding pattern. We circled the airport for 30 minutes until a runway opened up. The moment it was clear, we got permission from the control tower to land.

The Holy Spirit does the same thing. He hovers—waiting in a holding pattern—until He gets permission to land. The control tower for your life is your mouth.

The Holy Spirit will not force Himself on you. He's waiting for clearance. But the moment you say, "Jesus, baptize me in the Holy Spirit," you've cleared the runway—and He comes upon you.

RECEIVE

In Scripture, the most common way people received the baptism in the Holy Spirit was through the laying on of hands.

We see this in **Acts 8**, when Peter and John laid hands on the believers in Samaria. In **Acts 9**, Ananias laid hands on Paul. In **Acts 19**, Paul laid hands on a group of disciples in Ephesus. In each case, someone physically laid hands on them and prayed, and they received the Holy Spirit.

Now, that's not the only way. In **Acts 10**, when Peter was preaching at Cornelius' house, the Holy Spirit fell on everyone *while he was still preaching*. Nobody laid hands on them—they just received.

Is the laying on of hands required? No. But it is the *most common way*. However, regardless of the method, receiving the Holy Spirit isn't passive. It requires your participation.

In Acts 1:8, Jesus said, *"You shall receive power when the Holy Spirit has come upon you."* The word for *receive* there is the Greek word *lambano*, which means "to take, to grasp, to lay hold of."[1] The word implies a personal, active involvement rather than a passive reception. It's not waiting with arms crossed; it's reaching out with open hands.

This is where many people miss it. They take a passive posture toward receiving the Holy Spirit.

Americans, in particular, love being passive. We love sitting, and we don't like standing. Think about it: we have chairs in every room except the bedroom because when we are tired of sitting, we lie down.

Think about it: the car, the train, and the airplane? All just moving chairs. One of the first games we learned as kids? *Musical chairs*. It's a game that is all about the importance of finding a chair. When someone commits a terrible crime, we give them the electric chair. We're gonna kill you, but we're not savages. Have a seat.

We love to sit so much that it's illegal to stand around. It's called loitering. It's against the law to stand around because we have no idea why anyone would be in an area without chairs.

That's why a standing ovation is such a big deal in this country. If you can get someone out of their chair to cheer for you, that is quite an accomplishment. Let's be honest: Americans are lazy; we love to sit.

And that mindset leaks into our spirituality. Many people have a lazy, passive attitude toward receiving the Holy Spirit and speaking in tongues.

Too many believers are sitting back, spiritually speaking, saying, "If God wants me to have the Holy Spirit, He knows where to find me, but I'm not going to seek after it."

The Bible is clear: God wants you to receive it, but you have to actively take hold of it. God is looking for hunger, not apathy. Receiving the Spirit isn't about being worthy—it's about being thirsty.

Jesus said it like this:

> On the last day, that great day of the feast, Jesus stood and cried out, saying, "If anyone thirsts, let him come to Me and drink. He who believes in Me, as the Scripture has said, out of his heart will flow rivers of living water." But this He spoke concerning the Spirit, whom those believing in Him would receive; for the Holy Spirit was not yet given, because Jesus was not yet glorified.
>
> JOHN 7:37-39 NKJV

Jesus used the illustration of drinking water to receiving the Holy Spirit. If you want to receive the Holy Spirit, you need to be thirsty. You don't have to be perfect; you don't have to have all the sin out of your life. Your theology doesn't have to be flawless; you just have to be thirsty.

If you aren't thirsty, you won't receive it. The requirement for receiving the Holy Spirit is thirst. Jesus said, "If anyone is thirsty, come drink." You have to seek it, crave it, and desire it like you would water in the middle of the desert.

I grew up in Las Vegas—a concrete desert in the middle of an actual desert. Summers in Vegas hit 115 degrees. There is a bank sign with the time and temperature on it, and at one time, it said, "Time 1:16. Temperature 116 at the same." I thought, "I hope it's not the same at 4: 30."

It's hot in the desert. Whenever I tell people in the South about the heat in Las Vegas, they say, "Yeah, but it's dry heat." So is an oven. Why don't you stick your head in one and see how it feels?

When you are in the desert, water is a precious commodity. You desire it more than anything else. If you want to receive the Holy Spirit, you need to thirst for Him like water in the desert.

If you seek after the Holy Spirit like water in the desert and if you are thirsty for Him, you will receive!

RELEASE

After you've asked God to baptize you in the Holy Spirit and have had someone lay hands on you and pray, the only thing left to do is **release your prayer language**.

And this is where a lot of people get stuck.

They're waiting for the Holy Spirit to completely take over and start moving their mouth—like they're going to be overtaken and suddenly blurt out words without any effort. But that's not how it works.

When I received the baptism in the Holy Spirit, I struggled to speak in tongues. I could feel God's tangible presence like never before. His love and power were so real that I knew something supernatural was happening. But… nothing was coming out of my mouth.

I turned to my friend who was praying for me and said, "It's not working. Nothing's happening." He said, "The Holy Spirit isn't going to take control of your mouth and make you speak in another language."

I hadn't yet realized—**I had to do the speaking.** I thought the Holy Spirit was going to speak for me. But it doesn't work that way. You have to use your own vocal cords and speak out.

And **they** were all filled with the Holy Spirit and began to speak in other tongues as the Spirit gave **them** utterance.

ACTS 2:4 NKJV (Emphasis Added)

Who did the speaking? They did. The Holy Spirit gave them the utterance, but they did the speaking.

The speaking part is not supernatural. It's natural. The utterance is supernatural because it comes from the Spirit. But speaking? That's on you.

Every supernatural act in Scripture has two parts: God's part and your part.

Moses stretched out his hand—
God parted the sea (Exodus 14:21).

Peter stepped out of the boat—
God kept him above the waves (Matthew 14:29).

The Israelites marched around Jericho—
God brought the walls down (Joshua 6:1–20).

With every miracle, there is the natural part and the supernatural part. So, while God's power accomplishes the supernatural, He requires us to do the natural. When it comes to speaking in tongues, you have to do the natural and speak, and as you speak, God gives the supernatural utterance.

This means you'll have to use your tongue, your lungs, and your vocal cords. You have to make the effort to speak just as you would if you were speaking in your native language. The speaking part is natural; it's where the utterance comes from that makes it supernatural. It's not coming from your mind; it's coming from the Spirit.

The way it happens for many people is that a phrase or word that doesn't make sense will come to their mind, and they'll speak it out. For others, their lips stammer, and they'll begin to speak. For some people, their tongue will quiver as they begin to speak, and some don't feel or hear anything; they just speak out in faith. It's different for every person, but the main thing is you have to speak. God will not do the speaking for you.

God is not going to make you speak. God will not reach into your mouth and force you to talk like a puppet. He won't violate your will and make you vocalize another language.

You will have to make a conscious decision to pray in an unknown language. You must decide to pray in tongues by partnering in faith with the Holy Spirit. Although speaking is a function of the Spirit, it is activated by your faith and obedience.

Receiving the Holy Spirit isn't complicated, but it does require a response. Ask in faith, come thirsty, and be willing to release what God gives you. You don't have to strive or wait—He's already been poured out. All that's left is for you to receive, respond, and step into the supernatural life Jesus made possible.

HOLY SPIRIT GIVES THE SUPERNATURAL UTTERANCE, BUT HE WILL NOT DO THE SPEAKING FOR YOU.

CHAPTER 13

TONGUE-TIED

There was an ice factory that caught fire. Yes, you read that right—an ice factory. They had to call the fire department to put out the flames even though the factory was filled with all the water they needed. The problem? All their assets were frozen.

When you are baptized in the Holy Spirit, you receive the gift of tongues. You have everything you need to speak in tongues. The problem is that many people's assets are still frozen. They don't know how to get this gift active and working in their lives.

What's keeping people from releasing their prayer language? Here are four of **the most common hindrances to speaking in tongues.**

1. PRIDE

Have you ever done something that made you look ridiculous? Like walking up a flight of stairs and thinking there's one more step, only to nearly fall on your face. You end up looking like a baby giraffe trying to walk for the first time.

Or when you're on an elevator and you get off on the wrong floor, so you have to walk back in. I feel like I owe everyone an explanation for what happened. "Sorry, I thought it was the 5th floor. Everything looks exactly the same except for that giant number 2 on the wall."

The worst is when you walk into a spiderweb because no one else can see the spiderweb. You're walking along, and everything is fine, and then you freak out. You just look like you're losing your mind or fighting off a swarm of bees. You look ridiculous.

Here's the point: we've all done things that made us look silly. But for some reason, when it comes to spiritual things, we get really protective of our dignity.

Many people don't release their prayer language because they are worried about looking and sounding foolish. You will have to humble yourself if you want to pray in tongues because you will feel absolutely ridiculous when you speak out words you don't understand. Every person I've prayed for to receive the baptism of the Holy Spirit felt foolish when they first started.

Speaking in tongues is the language of humility. It forces you to humble yourself and surrender your intellect and understanding to the Holy Spirit. When you pray in tongues, you empty yourself of your ego and pride as you allow the Holy Spirit to pray through you.

There was a man who heard about the baptism in the Holy Spirit at his church. He even had people pray for him to receive it, but he didn't yield. He couldn't quite get past the mental barrier.

A few months later, his wife was smiling one morning while he was getting ready. He asked her why, and she said, "I don't want to embarrass you." He pressed her, and she finally told him, "I couldn't sleep last night, so I got up to read. When I came back to bed, I heard you speaking in tongues in your sleep."

He was shocked. "I wasn't speaking in tongues. I was asleep!"

She said, "Nope. You were praying in tongues."

He went to his pastor and asked, "Is it possible to speak in tongues in your sleep?"

The pastor smiled and said, "Oh yeah. Happens to a lot of hard-headed people."

Don't be hard-headed and prideful; humble yourself and release your prayer language.

2. FEAR

Some people are afraid to speak in tongues because they think they might lose control. They're worried they'll be standing in a silent elevator with five strangers and suddenly erupt in tongues—only for someone to hit the emergency button thinking you're having a seizure.

But let me put your mind at ease—you are in complete control of this gift. First Corinthians 14 is basically a user's manual for operating in tongues appropriately. Paul addresses when to speak in tongues and when to keep silent. If Paul gives instructions on when to use the gift and when to remain silent, it proves that you have full control over its operation.

Other people fear they'll "mess it up." They think, What if I don't do it right? What if I sound silly? What if it's just me?

Here's the good news: even if it is a little messy at first, your heavenly Father still loves it.

Tongues is a language. No one is fluent in a new language the first time they speak it. Your first words weren't eloquent—they were "Mama" and "Dada." You probably said "pasghetti" instead of spaghetti. Yet, we celebrate toddlers just for trying to talk. Don't worry about whether or not you do it perfectly. Your heavenly Father loves to hear you.

3. OVERTHINKING

This is one of the most common hang-ups when it comes to praying in tongues. People step out in faith, start speaking, and then immediately think, "I don't think that was God. I think that was just me."

The reason you feel like it's you is because *it is you*. Obviously, it's not *all* you, but it's not all God, either. It's you and the Holy Spirit together.

It always amazes me when people think they are cool for driving fast as they zoom you. That doesn't make you cool; everybody knows it's not you who is going fast; it's the car. Even when people talk about driving, they say, "I was going 90 mph." No, the car was going 90 mph because you pushed the pedal down 5 inches.

That's how praying in tongues works. You push the pedal by speaking, and Holy Spirit horsepower kicks in as He gives you the utterance. But if you don't push the pedal, it won't engage the engine, and nothing will happen.

When you speak in tongues, it will feel like it's you because you are the one doing the speaking, but it's the Holy Spirit who inspires your speech.

If while you are praying in tongues, you are also thinking, "This isn't God, it's just me." It's proof you're speaking in tongues because if you are thinking that thought while at the same time speaking in an unknown language, you are praying tongues.

In order to speak in your native language, you have to think about what you are saying, but when you speak in tongues, your mind can be thinking about one thing while you're saying something else. So if while you're praying in tongues, you're thinking words like, "This isn't God, it's me." It's proof you're praying in tongues. If you're praying while doubting at the same time, congratulations—you're officially speaking in tongues.

Bottom line: If it feels like you, it's because it is you in part, so don't overthink it.

4. INACTION

> What is the conclusion then? I will pray with the spirit, and I will also pray with the understanding. I will sing with the spirit, and I will also sing with the understanding.
>
> 1 CORINTHIANS 14:15 NKJV

Notice Paul says, "I will pray with the spirit, and I will pray with the understanding." That means praying in the Spirit is a decision. Just like praying in English is a choice, praying in tongues is an act of the will.

Speaking in tongues is a conscious decision you make just like every other time you pray which means you will have to open up your mouth and speak. But for some reason, when it comes to speaking in tongues, people will stand their mouths closed, lips locked, waiting for the Holy Spirit to hijack their mouth and start speaking for them, like they're expecting a divine ventriloquist moment.

God doesn't do that when you pray over your dinner. If I'm halfway through a plate of tacos and suddenly remember I didn't pray, God doesn't reach down, grab my jaw, and make me say, "God is great, God is good, let us thank Him for our food..." That has literally never happened.

Every time I've prayed—even something as routine as blessing my food—it's required me to open my mouth and speak. Same with tongues. I've been praying in tongues for over 20 years, and not once has God taken over and made me do it. Every time, it started with a choice: I will pray in the Spirit.

Yet for some reason, when it comes to tongues, people expect the Holy Spirit to do all the work. I've heard folks say, "If I ever speak in tongues, it won't be me." Now, if what they mean is they're not going to fake it, that's fine. But if they mean the Holy Spirit is going to control their vocal cords and start speaking through them like a puppet, they've misunderstood how this works.

Imagine if that's how we treated every gift of the spirit. How do you know you have the gift of giving? Well, I was walking by the offering box by the door, and $20 jumped out of my wallet and into the box. No, even if you have the gift of giving, you still have to pull out your checkbook and write a check.

How did you discover you had the gift of healing? Well, I was walking by this sick person, and my hand suddenly went on their shoulder, and I started praying for healing. No, you stepped out in faith and laid hands on someone and prayed for them to be healed.

There is no spiritual gift that is all Holy Spirit; every gift of the Spirit is a cooperation between you and the Holy Spirit. You step out in faith, and the Holy Spirit meets you at the place of faith.

You do the natural and He adds His super to your natural. It's the same way with tongues. You step out in faith and speak and He gives the supernatural utterance, but He will not do the speaking for you.

If you've been waiting for God to suddenly take control of your mouth and do it all for you, that's not how it works. If you want to speak in tongues, you have to make the conscious decision to open your mouth and speak. God won't speak for you, but if you open your mouth and speak, He will inspire your speech.

Now, if you are going to speak, you have to use your voice. I want you to use your voice without saying an actual word. Don't worry I'm not going to do the repeat after me really fast, *"I should have bought a Honda but instead I bought a Kia."*

I want you to use your voice without using words. Make the sound "Aaahhh." Go ahead. Do it out loud. I'll wait.

You will have to do at least that if you want to speak in tongues. God will not possess your vocal cords and make sounds come out. You speak, He gives you the utterance.

If you don't speak, nothing will happen. You can pray, beg, tarry, wait, and have everyone you know lay hands on you, but if you don't open your mouth and speak, nothing will happen.

You do the natural and He adds His super to your natural.

The mechanics of speaking in tongues are not supernatural. You have to open your mouth, use your voice, and speak, just like you would if you were speaking in your native language. The supernatural part is that the utterance doesn't come from your natural mind; it comes from your spirit as you speak.

Speaking in tongues is a language of faith. Your part is to release sounds and syllables and trust that He will add the meaning and intention behind those words.

Everything we receive from God is by faith. We receive salvation by faith. We receive forgiveness by faith. We receive healing by faith. Everything comes through faith, but when it comes to tongues, we think God is doing it all, so faith isn't required.

But It takes faith to speak in tongues. It takes faith to release words you don't understand, trusting the Holy Spirit to pray through you. Many have no problem trusting God for salvation, finances, or healing, but they don't have the faith to step out and speak in tongues.

If you don't step out in faith and speak, nothing will happen. You can have water piped into your house, but if you don't turn on the faucet, nothing will come out. The same is true when it comes to tongues. This gift is given when you're baptized in the Spirit, but if you don't open your mouth and speak, nothing will come out. However, if you step out in faith and speak, God will inspire your words and pray through you.

A pastor once told the story of praying with a friend who was speaking in tongues. His friend sounded like a character from a *Star Wars* movie when he spoke in tongues: "Bop wop nop dop." At the time, the pastor didn't pray in tongues. He believed in it, and he heard other people pray in tongues, and it sounded beautiful, but when his friend prayed, it sounded terrible. He started laughing on the inside, thinking, "This guy's not very good at this."

But then the Holy Spirit spoke to him and said, "At least he has the courage to try."

That's what I want to leave you with: have the courage to try. It's okay if it doesn't sound polished. It's okay if it feels awkward. God isn't listening for perfection—He's listening for faith. Open your mouth. Speak. Trust the Holy Spirit to give the utterance.

CONCLUSION

When I was baptized in the Holy Spirit, I felt the tangible presence of God in such a powerful way. I felt God's power and love coursing through every part of my body. Although I initially struggled to speak in tongues, it was easy once I stepped out in faith—especially since God's presence was upon me in such an overwhelming way. There was no doubt that I was baptized in the Spirit and spoke in tongues.

However, the next morning, I didn't sense the tangible presence of God in the same way. God's power wasn't coursing through me like it was the day before. I didn't have the same awareness of His love that had felt so present the day before. And because I wasn't experiencing all the same physical manifestations, it wasn't as easy to pray in tongues.

It felt like I was forcing it—or worse, just making it up. So I stopped. In fact, after my initial experience of being filled with the Spirit, I didn't speak in tongues for months. I kept waiting for the same feeling to come back so I could speak in tongues again—but it never did. I was relying on my feelings instead of my faith. What I didn't realize at the time was that any time I wanted to speak in tongues, I could. I just had to step out in faith and speak, and the Holy Spirit would give me the utterance.

While your experience of being immersed in the Spirit of God may come with tangible manifestations of His presence and power, don't connect the gift of tongues to that feeling. This is a gift of the Spirit you can step into regardless of how you feel. Just like turning on a faucet at your house, it's an act of the will—something you can choose to do, whether or not the emotions are there in the moment.

You don't always feel something when you pray in your native language. You don't always get goosebumps when you read your Bible. You don't always feel God's tangible presence when you worship—but that doesn't stop you from engaging in those spiritual disciplines. The same is true with speaking in tongues. It's more a discipline to practice than a feeling you experience.

Don't let this gift sit dormant in your life just because you don't feel God's presence. This gift isn't activated by feelings—it's activated by faith. Don't allow the enemy to convince you that it's just you, or that you're making things up. Press through the mental battles and exercise this gift until it becomes a normal part of your prayer life.

And if you're ready to receive the baptism in the Holy Spirit, there's a simple prayer included in the Appendix at the end of this book. Use it as a starting point. Let it guide your words, but more importantly—let it guide your faith. The Holy Spirit is hovering. He's ready. He's just waiting for you to open your mouth and give Him permission to land.

APPENDIX

If you're ready to receive the baptism in the Holy Spirit, this prayer is here to guide you.

You don't have to earn it. You don't have to work for it. You simply receive it by faith—just like salvation. The Holy Spirit is already hovering, waiting for your invitation. All He needs is permission.

Whether this is your first time praying about this or you've been seeking it for years, come thirsty. Come expectant. Come ready to speak by faith.

Use this prayer as a guide. Say it out loud. Make it personal. And then—speak. Let the gift flow.

PRAYER FOR THE BAPTISM IN THE HOLY SPIRIT

Heavenly Father,

I come to You in the name of Jesus, Your Son. Thank You for the gift of salvation. I declare that Jesus Christ is my Lord, and I believe in His finished work on the cross for the forgiveness of my sins. Because of His blood, I now come boldly before You, asking for the gift

You promised to all who believe in Your name—the gift of the Holy Spirit.

Lord, I recognize that the baptism in the Holy Spirit is a gift. It's not something I can earn or deserve. I receive it by faith, just as I received salvation. Your Word says that if we ask, we will receive, and I believe that promise is for me today.

So now, I ask You to baptize me in the Holy Spirit. Fill me from the top of my head to the soles of my feet. I open my heart fully to You and ask You to clothe me with power from on high. Let Your Spirit come upon me in power. Fill me to overflowing so I can be a vessel for Your glory and a bold witness for Jesus.

Lord Jesus, just as You baptized Your disciples on the Day of Pentecost, baptize me now. By faith, I receive the fullness of the Holy Spirit. I trust You to give me the gifts You've promised. I yield my tongue to You and ask You to give me words of prayer and praise that come directly from Your Spirit.

I receive this baptism by faith, and I thank You for it right now. I believe I am filled with the Holy Spirit, and I will walk in the power and authority You've given me, in the mighty name of Jesus.

Amen.

SOURCES

Greek word studies are based on: Strong, James. (1890). Strong's Exhaustive Concordance of the Bible. Abingdon Press. Lexical entries accessed via BibleStudyTools.com.

INTRODUCTION

1. *Dunamis* – Strong's G1411

CHAPTER 2

1. *Baptó* – Strong's G911

2. *Baptizo* – Strong's G907

3. Nicander of Colophon. Recipe for pickling, as quoted in Athenaeus, Deipnosophistae, Book 4, 133d

CHAPTER 3

1. *Emphysaō* – Strong's G1720

CHAPTER 4

1. *Epipiptō* – Strong's G1968

CHAPTER 7

1. *Glossa* – Strong's G1100

2. *Logos* – Strong's G3056

CHAPTER 11

1. Restore. Merriam-Webster Dictionary.

CHAPTER 12

1. *Lambano* – Strong's G2983

Additional books from Joshua Copron available on Amazon.

In *Graceology*, Joshua Copron unpacks what it means to live out of the "manifold grace of God" and how a deeper understanding of God's grace brings the promise of unparalleled freedom.

Graceology is not just another book about grace. It is an in-depth look at the limitless subject that anchors us to our divine creator. This knowledge of grace not only transforms who we are, but leads us into the abundant life God has for each of us.

Do you feel like you're trapped in cycles of uncontrollable emotions? Do joy, patience, and self control feel out of reach in your everyday life? Do your feelings end up robbing you of the peace you long for?

Feel Free is a practical guide to discovering the role emotions are designed to play and how to conquer the destructive emotions that have held you back.

Untangled gives you Biblical strategies to overcome toxic emotions and unlock the full potential of your life.

The road to freedom is not always easy, yet with this practical guide you can develop the habits, rhythms, relationships, and thought patterns you need to thrive in a world that tries to keep you down. Don't let your negative emotions control you any longer. It's time to get Untangled.

Do you ever feel like your life is aimless? Do you dream of making a lasting impact? Do you fear succeeding at things that don't really matter in eternity?

Your presence on this planet means you have a purpose, but how do you know what that purpose is? In *Discover Purpose* you will find a practical path to identifying your God-given purpose and how to walk in the fullness of His plan for your life.

The world operates according to the law of seed time and harvest, and not just in nature. Your life is the harvest of seeds sewn. Learn how your faith and actions can unlock a life filled with joy, purpose, and abundance.

Create Your Future unpacks the timeless truth of harvest with powerfully fresh and practical insight. It is time to dream bigger and sow seeds strategically to create your future.

God's promises are clear: He will exceed abundantly above all we ask or imagine. But here's the catch – He's waiting for us to ask! This book reveals the profound truth that God responds to our bold requests.

This book isn't just about theory – it's a practical guide to cultivating a lifestyle of great faith. Discover how you can transform lives, release miracles, and move mountains through the power of your *Big Ask!*

Feeling stuck? Waiting for a "perfect" moment to step into God's calling? The Path to Purpose provides a map to overcome the barriers of indecision, fear, procrastination, and even the distractions of daily life.

With its powerful mix of encouragement, humor, and practical advice, Joshua Copron reminds us that clarity comes in the going, not in the waiting. Discover how to get off the sidelines and start successfully navigating your destiny!

Made in the USA
Columbia, SC
01 June 2025

58771259R00091